New Directions for
Student Services

John H. Schuh
EDITOR-IN-CHIEF

Elizabeth J. Whitt
ASSOCIATE EDITOR

Biracial and Multiracial Students

Kristen A. Renn
Paul Shang
EDITORS

D1524289

Number 123 • Fall 2008
Jossey-Bass
San Francisco

BIRACIAL AND MULTIRACIAL STUDENTS
Kristen A. Renn, Paul Shang (eds.)
New Directions for Student Services, no. 123
John H. Schuh, Editor-in-Chief
Elizabeth J. Whitt, Associate Editor

NEW DIRECTIONS FOR STUDENT SERVICES (ISSN 0164-7970, e-ISSN 1536-0695) is part of The Jossey-Bass Higher and Adult Education Series and is published quarterly by Wiley Subscription Services, Inc., A Wiley Company, at Jossey-Bass, 989 Market Street, San Francisco, California 94103-1741. Periodicals Postage Paid at San Francisco, California, and at additional mailing offices. POSTMASTER: Send address changes to New Directions for Student Services, Jossey-Bass, 989 Market Street, San Francisco, CA 94103-1741.

New Directions for Student Services is indexed in CIJE: Current Index to Journals in Education (ERIC), Contents Pages in Education (T&F), Current Abstracts (EBSCO), Education Index/Abstracts (H.W. Wilson), Educational Research Abstracts Online (T&F), ERIC Database (Education Resources Information Center), and Higher Education Abstracts (Claremont Graduate University).

Microfilm copies of issues and articles are available in 16mm and 35mm, as well as microfiche in 105mm, through University Microfilms Inc., 300 North Zeeb Road, Ann Arbor, Michigan 48106-1346.

SUBSCRIPTIONS cost $89 for individuals and $228 for institutions, agencies, and libraries in the United States. See ordering information page at end of book.

EDITORIAL CORRESPONDENCE should be sent to the Editor-in-Chief, John H. Schuh, N 243 Lagomarcino Hall, Iowa State University, Ames, Iowa 50011.

www.josseybass.com

29.60

Contents

Editors' Notes

Student affairs educators have observed an increase in the number of biracial and multiracial college students, defined as students who have parents from more than one federally defined racial or ethnic background, such as Asian-White, Latino-Black, or Native-White-Latino (Talbot, Gasser, Kellogg, and Stubbs, 2006), and data from the U.S. Census Bureau (Jones and Smith, 2001) predict a steady increase in this population over time. A substantial amount of literature, including several volumes of *New Directions for Student Services* (McEwen and others, 2002; Ortiz, 2004; Tippeconic Fox, Lowe, and McClellan, 2005), addresses developmental and service needs of monoracial students of color (Asian and Pacific Islander, Black, Latino, and Native American), but student affairs professionals have few resources on which to draw in understanding the experiences and identities of traditional-age multiracial students. We intend this volume to meet this need.

In the past five years, a small body of empirical research on multiracial college students (for example, Kellogg, 2006; Renn, 2004; Talbot, Gasser, Kellogg, and Stubbs, 2006) has emerged that is being used in service of this growing population. Our goals here are to expand the reach of this research and share examples of good practice in providing programs and services for multiracial students, also known as mixed-race or mixed-heritage students. We also aim to expand consideration of biracial and multiracial issues to include bicultural faculty members and mixed-race Canadians.

Evidence of the need for knowledge about multiracial students comes in the form of robust attendance at professional conference sessions on serving multiracial students and from the many requests for information that we who present on these topics receive, as well as the establishment in 2005 of the MultiRacial Network in the American College Personnel Association Commission on Multicultural Affairs. Further evidence of interest in this topic comes from multiracial students themselves, who at regional and national conferences of mixed race students (2004 National Conference on the Mixed Race Experience, held at the Claremont Colleges; 2006 National Conference on the Mixed Race Experience, held at Macalester College) call on their institutions to understand their needs and to provide appropriate services on campus (see Campus Awareness & Compliance Initiative, 2005). We have attempted to meet the interests of all of these groups, though we recognize that in an area as dynamic and growing as multiracial student research and practice, it is nearly impossible to stay ahead of developments in the field. We designed this volume to be used in its entirety to

New Directions for Student Services, no. 123, Fall 2008 © Wiley Periodicals, Inc.
Published online in Wiley InterScience (www.interscience.wiley.com) • DOI: 10.1002/ss.280

1

provide broad coverage of important aspects of theory and practice and as individual chapters for readers who are interested in understanding one or more aspects in depth.

In Chapter One, Paul Shang provides an introduction to the complexities of race and racial identity in the United States and on campus. He points out where we have, and perhaps have not, made progress in understanding race and race relations in the past several decades.

Kristen Renn describes in Chapter Two various models of identity development for biracial youth and college students. She discusses how these models have been used in research and as the basis for services for students.

In Chapter Three, Donna Talbot describes original research findings on the development of students whose parents are both people of color. In comparison with mixed-race students who have one parent who is White, these students may have greater difficulties identifying with a peer group and experience more personal isolation. Talbot explores how they are confronted by the challenges of addressing intragroup dynamics without the privileges associated with having a White heritage.

The challenges and joys of being a biracial student are described by Alissa King in Chapter Four, in which she shares data from her research, other research on biracial students, and her own experiences addressing the perennial *Who am I?* and *What are you?* questions that college students explore.

Michael Paul Wong and Joshua Buckner in Chapter Five and C. Casey Ozaki and Marc Johnston in Chapter Six discuss providing services to multiracial students. Wong and Buckner provide an overview of services developed within the context of multicultural affairs or minority affairs offices that have branched out to include providing services to mixed-race students. Given that the history of providing services to students of color has been based on serving monoracial students, the development of services for mixed-race students has featured a variety of approaches. Related to the dearth of organized services for mixed-race students, Ozaki and Johnston emphasize the role that student organizations play for identity development, emotional support, and organizing around social and intellectual causes. Ozaki and Johnston also provide ten recommendations for advisers working with organizations of multiracial students.

In Chapter Seven, Heather Shea Gasser explores the use of technology by multiracial students to form relationships, gain affirmation, and develop personally. She provides a number of online resources and discusses the imperative for student affairs professionals to be familiar with technology and how to use it to serve students.

In Chapter Eight, Michael Cuyjet describes the experience of being bicultural, in comparison to being biracial or multiracial, and juxtaposes the bicultural experience with the values of the predominant culture. He compares the perspectives of being a bicultural faculty member and establishing faculty identity with the traditional values ascribed to faculty culture. In so doing, he not only depicts the challenges bicultural faculty experience in their academic departments, but also represents the importance of demonstrating the successful bicultural experience for all students, especially students of color.

Leanne Taylor provides an international perspective, specifically Canadian, in Chapter Nine. Although the Canadian outlook on and history of racial matters differs from that of the United States, Taylor points out that mixed-race people in Canada have experiences that are similar to those in the United States. We include this chapter to provide an alternative perspective on understanding race from outside the United States and to inform student affairs professionals who practice in other nations.

In Chapter Ten Angela Kellogg and Amanda Niskodé describe how U.S. higher education institutions must adapt to recent changes in federal policy that require them to collect and report data on race/ethnicity in a format that allows students to identify themselves in multiple categories. They discuss implications of this shift for admissions policies and other policies designed to build diverse student bodies. Kellogg and Niskodé also underscore one of the themes of this volume: serving all students well may begin by allowing them to identify themselves accurately. Serving all students well requires the recognition, appreciation, and understanding of their diverse backgrounds and the acknowledgment of their experiences in the whole of higher education.

References

Campus Awareness and Compliance Initiative. *CACI Toolkit*, 2005. Retrieved May 14, 2006, from *http://www.mixituponcampus.org/*

Jones, N. A., and Smith, A. S. "The Two or More Races Population: 2000." Washington, D.C.: U.S. Census Bureau, 2001.

Kellogg, A. H. "Exploring Critical Incidents in the Racial Identity of Multiracial College Students." Unpublished doctoral dissertation, University of Iowa, 2006.

McEwen, M. K., and others (eds.). *Working with Asian American College Students*. New Directions for Student Services, no. 97. San Francisco: Jossey-Bass, 2002.

Ortiz, A. M. (ed.). *Addressing the Unique Needs of Latino American Students*. New Directions for Student Services, no. 105. San Francisco: Jossey-Bass, 2004.

Renn, K. A. *Mixed Race Students in College: The Ecology of Race, Identity, and Community*. Albany, N.Y.: SUNY Press, 2004.

Talbot, D. M., Gasser, H., Kellogg, A., and Stubbs, L. "Understanding and Enhancing the Educational Experience for Mixed-Race Students." Paper presented at the ACPA Annual Convention, Indianapolis, Ind., 2006.

Tippeconnic Fox, M. J., Lowe, S. C., and McClellan, G. S. (eds.). *Serving Native American Students*. New Directions for Student Services, no. 109. San Francisco: Jossey-Bass, 2005.

Kristen A. Renn
Paul Shang
Editors

KRISTEN A. RENN is associate professor of higher, adult, and lifelong education at Michigan State University.

PAUL SHANG is assistant vice chancellor for student development at the University of Missouri-Kansas City and a past president of ACPA—College Student Educators International.

1

This chapter describes social and historical developments coinciding with the emergence of increasing numbers of biracial and multiracial college students. It thus sets the context for the chapters that follow on identity development, student experiences, student services, and policy.

An Introduction to Social and Historical Factors Affecting Multiracial College Students

Paul Shang

Biracial and multiracial college students—students having parents from more than one racial/ethnic category—are coming to campus in increasing numbers (Jaschik, 2006). This chapter introduces social and historical factors that affect the experiences of multiracial students and describes social and political developments that may have an impact on how colleges and universities serve this mixed-race population. I first set a context for understanding biracial students as students of color in the twenty-first century. Second, I argue that multiracial and biracial people in the United States historically have been treated in ways that college student services providers should consider. Finally, I describe the ways that the characteristics of current students and their precollege socialization about racial issues may be important in the development of services and approaches for serving multiracial and biracial students—and all other students as well.

The Post–Affirmative Action Era

The late Dr. Martin Luther King Jr. could have been describing race and race relations in the United States in 2008 rather than in 1968 when he spoke at Ohio Northern University and said: "So in order to tell the truth, it is necessary to move on, not simply talk about the fact that we've made strides,

NEW DIRECTIONS FOR STUDENT SERVICES, no. 123, Fall 2008 © Wiley Periodicals, Inc.
Published online in Wiley InterScience (www.interscience.wiley.com) • DOI: 10.1002/ss.281

but honestly face the fact that we have a long, long way to go before the problem of racial injustice is solved in our country" (King, 1968, p. 34).

Multiracial students attend college at a time when problems of racial injustice remain unsolved. They attend college during the post–affirmative action era, so-called by the media and scholars because the use of race in college admissions has been banned by the electorate in some states (among them, California, Michigan, and Washington) and through legal or governmental processes in others (including Texas and Florida). President George W. Bush criticized the use of race in college admissions, calling the practice "divisive" and "unfair" (Bush, 2003, p. 4), and public debate and media focus on issues of college admissions, race, racism, and inequality (Stein, 1995).

Contributing to the sense that problems of racial injustice remain unsolved are indicators that whatever progress may have been made during the civil rights era is, at best, now stalled. In 2000, almost a third more African American men were in prison than enrolled in college (Ziedenberg and Schiraldi, 2002). Schools in the United States are becoming more segregated rather than less (Orfield and Lee, 2007). For 2006, the Federal Bureau of Investigation reported an 8 percent increase in hate crimes, of which over half were racially motivated (CNN, 2007). According to a Pew Research Center and National Public Radio poll conducted in fall 2007, only 20 percent of black Americans said that black Americans were better off than they were five years ago. No poll has reported as low as 20 percent since 1983 during Ronald Reagan's first term as president (NPR, 2007). The preponderance of evidence suggests that in the United States, the playing field is not level for people of all races.

In addition to the comparatively polite, intellectual public debate about race and equality, people of color continue to be the target of personal, racially based insults. Don Imus's infamous reference to the Rutgers women's basketball team as "nappy headed hos" on his nationally syndicated radio program *Imus in the Morning* (Associated Press, 2007) is an example of the racial bigotry that many people may still harbor privately but are unwilling to express except indirectly and through innuendo. However, as Stein (1995) pointed out, great hostility exists toward attempts to address the discrimination of the past through efforts considered to be preferential, and this antipathy becomes even more pronounced when the economy is weak.

It is in these larger social and historical contexts that biracial students attend college. Widely disparate perspectives on the use of race as a factor in college admissions and broader questions about the achievement of a level playing field by members of different races are examples of the nation's attempt to work out the unresolved issues of race that King (1968) predicted would persist. Student services practitioners operate in this context and must be aware of these ongoing debates, mindful of the political ideology that might appear to be represented, intentionally or not, in their services.

NEW DIRECTIONS FOR STUDENT SERVICES • DOI: 10.1002/ss

Biracial and Multiracial Students in the United States

Of the 6.8 million people who indicated more than one racial category on the 2000 U.S. Census, 40 percent were under eighteen years old, predicting an increase in the number of multiracial students attending higher education in the coming years (Jaschik, 2006). Further evidence for the predicted increase in multiracial students is provided by an increase in interracial marriages from less than 2 percent in 1970 to more than 7 percent of 59 million married couples in 2005 (cited by Crary, 2007), and the impact of immigration as well as transracial and international adoption. How biracial or multiracial students feel about themselves and how they interpret their treatment by others is complicated not only by the nation's current debate about responding to historical wrongs based on race, but also by the nation's ambivalence about mixed-race people (Root, 1996). In 2008, mixed-race public figures abound: Tiger Woods, Vin Diesel, Dwayne "The Rock" Johnson, Halle Berry, Soledad O'Brien, Derek Jeter, and Barack Obama are just a few. Yet mixed-race people, and the families from which they came, were not welcome in many parts of the United States just a few generations ago.

The last state law banning interracial marriage—Alabama's—was repealed as recently as 2000 (Cruz and Berson, 2001), thirty-three years after the U.S. Supreme Court made its ruling in *Loving* v. *Virginia* that such laws were unconstitutional. At the time of the *Loving* decision, sixteen other states had laws similar to Virginia's banning miscegenation (Cruz and Berson, 2001). The *Loving* case began in 1958 when Mildred Delores Jeter (who is Black) and Richard Perry Loving (who is White) married in Washington, D.C., rather than in Virginia, where miscegenation was illegal (Nash, 1999). Several weeks after returning to Virginia, the Lovings were arrested in their bedroom: their marriage violated Virginia's 1924 Act to Preserve Racial Integrity (Nash, 1999). The U.S. Supreme Court agreed to hear the case of the Lovings, which had attracted the support of the National Association for the Advancement of Colored People, "a coalition of Catholic bishops, and the Japanese American Citizens League" (Nash, 1999, p. 165). The court found for the Lovings on June 12, 1967, and the grassroots Loving Day organization now celebrates the decision while also bringing awareness to the history of antimiscegenation laws in the United States.

Mixed-race couples such as John Rolfe and Pocahontas; Lewis and Clark expedition guides Sacajawea and her husband, Toussaint Charbonneau; abolitionist Frederick Douglass and his wife, Anna Murray; and entertainers Desi Arnaz and Lucille Ball, and their children, have always existed in the United States, along with entire communities consisting of mixed-race couples and children (Nash, 1999). Yet the proposition of loving someone from another race has been railed against from the pulpit and seen as morally degenerate or at least socially impractical (Nash, 1999) until recently. Thus, multiracial people are exposed to mixed messages about the acceptability of their heritages.

NEW DIRECTIONS FOR STUDENT SERVICES • DOI: 10.1002/ss

Recent polls indicate that especially among young people, attitudes in the United States toward interracial couples may be changing (Crary, 2007; Kassendorf and Nasser, 2001). This development might seem to be good news for multiracial college students. However, resistance to the recognition of biracial or multiracial individuals on the census or other government records has also drawn sharp criticism from monoracial groups that fear that the addition of more racial categories will diminish the numbers selecting one category (Holmes, 1996). Political groups representing African Americans, Asian and Pacific Islanders, and Hispanics, anxious to preserve hard-fought gains, are concerned about the importance of numbers for maintaining social services, the Voting Rights Act, and programs to increase representation in employment or higher education by underrepresented minority groups (Holmes, 1996).

Acceptance of mixed-race couples also may differ according to local and regional race relations and histories. Smothers (1994) reported on the controversy generated when a high school principal in Wedowee, Alabama, attempted to cancel the school prom because some students were planning to attend with a date of a different color. He also referred to one student with a Black mother and a White father as a "mistake," causing her to burst into tears. Some multiracial college students attended high schools such as this one, and others are exposed to these situations through the media.

For student services professionals, it is essential, as with all other students, to know each biracial or multiracial student as an individual, and it is important to bear in mind the change underway regarding the public's acceptance of mixed-race individuals and couples. How each biracial or multiracial individual understands the historic treatment and current context of mixed-race people is a factor to be considered in providing mentoring and other services to her or him (see Chapter Five, this volume).

The Diversity of New College Students

Traditional-age biracial and multiracial students are part of a cohort of students entering college at a time of great student diversity, yet they are likely to have little precollege experience with such diversity. For many college students, their first significant interaction with someone from another race occurs on campus (Millem and Umbach, 2003; Rankin and Reason, 2005). As researchers have noted (Howe and Strauss, 2000; Orfield and Lee, 2007), high schools are more segregated than they were before the 1980s, and more and more of the millennials, members of the generation born between 1982 and 2002 (Howe and Strauss, 2000), were home-schooled or attended independent schools or schools where parental spending has been organized "to end-run judicially imposed state equalization formulas" (Howe and Strauss, 2000, p. 106). This inexperience across races as well as the national debate over affirmative action and equity may be reflected in the Higher Education Research Institute finding that of entering freshmen responding in 2006, "only slightly more than one-third (34.0 percent) rated the objec-

tive of helping to promote racial understanding as 'essential' or 'very important,' a goal that has declined since it peaked in 1992 (46.4 percent), when
the Rodney King decision and riots in Los Angeles provoked national discussions about race" (Pryor and others, 2007, p. 8).

In the light of all these facts, it is a hopeful sign that in 2005, 11.6 percent more freshmen, on completion of their first year in college than at the
beginning, reported the personal goal of "helping to promote racial understanding" as being "very important" or "essential" (Hurtado and others,
2007, p. 23). Evidence suggests that this growth in awareness could result
from students' exposure to greater diversity on arrival at college and the
opportunities to interact with and learn from diverse student populations
(Pike, Kuh, and Gonyea, 2007).

Even as U.S. college and university educators ponder the impressive
changes occurring in the student body, they must also realize and plan for
the accommodation of this change as it manifests itself on campus (Broido,
2004). Not only will more students be attending college but more of them
will be students of color. According to Carnevale and Fry (2000), of the 2.6
million new students expected in 2015, 80 percent will be African American, Hispanic, and Asian or Pacific Islander, and minority students will com-
prise 37.2 percent of undergraduate enrollment. Increasing numbers of
multiracial students will be among them (Jaschik, 2006).

As more diverse students come to college from more segregated backgrounds, students may need more social support and opportunities to
explore personal backgrounds rather than less (Broido, 2004). The delivery
of these services, or opportunities, must be developed taking into consideration how contemporary college students access higher education in addition to their demographic characteristics. Students who transfer from one
institution to another, or "swirl" by enrolling back and forth between different institutions, or "double-dip" by attending several institutions at the same
time (McCormick 2003), present challenges for practitioners who are developing programs and activities with less dynamic, more traditional students
in mind. If Adelman (1999) is correct and over 60 percent of undergraduate
college students now attend more than one institution as they pursue their
degrees, those providing opportunities for students to explore diversity must
ensure the accessibility and appeal of their efforts to those whose attendance
on campus may be inconsistent. There is no evidence to suggest that multiracial students will swirl or double-dip at rates different from other students,
and so educators must assume that services for these students will also have
to meet the needs of the swirling, double-dipping masses.

Providing Programs and Services That Promote
Learning and Development

Evidence suggests that programs and services that are good for one group
of students, such as biracial and multiracial students, are often good for all

NEW DIRECTIONS FOR STUDENT SERVICES • DOI: 10.1002/ss

students (Pike and others, 2007; Smith and others, 1997). Higher education leaders must then clearly and forcefully articulate the stance that programs and services assisting students to understand racial and cultural diversity and to be comfortable in heterogeneous environments are a necessity for achieving success. As Smith and others noted:

> But diversity is finally not about the needs of one or another group competing for scarce resources. It is rather about purposeful and effective designs for supporting all students' educational achievement. As such, it is an integral component of the mission and purpose of the institution, and essential to whether our institutions are or will be positioned to educate all students for full participation in the economic, social, and civic domains of a diverse society [1997, p. 50].

Institutions of higher education remain great places for personal growth and development for students (Evans, Forney, and Guido-DiBrito, 1998). Judging from research on millennials (Broido, 2004; Howe and Strauss, 2000), colleges and universities remain an important place to meet people of different races, from different economic classes and countries, of different sexual orientations. Colleges and universities are places where personal questions such as those related to race and being biracial or multiracial are first confronted away from the support of family and communities (see Chapters Two through Four, this volume).

Programs and services for biracial and multiracial students should be provided with an understanding of current national dialogues about affirmative action and racial equity; social, legal, and historical contexts related to mixed-race people; and changing student populations in terms of demographics, generational characteristics, and attendance patterns. For student affairs professionals, the opportunity and the challenge to serve an ever-changing student body requires unremitting examination of the impact of services and institutional policies on students, how students achieve growth and development, and what promising new approaches may exist to serve students and the institution. Encouraged by serving biracial and multiracial students, faculty, staff, and other students may come to consider new ways of thinking about the fluidity of race or the diminishing usefulness of the concept of race; to learn and use new words like *phenotype, biracial, monoracial, multiracial, multicultural,* and *AHANA* (African, Hispanic, Asian, Native American); and to realize the impact of social norms and how profoundly societies can change. These concepts and others related to the experiences of being or serving biracial and multiracial students arise throughout this volume.

References

Adelman, C. *Answers in the Tool Box: Academic Intensity, Attendance Patterns, and Bachelor's Degree Attainment.* Jessup, Md.: U.S. Department of Education, 1999.

Associated Press. "NCAA, Rutgers Women's Coach Blasts Imus." Apr. 6, 2007. Retrieved Dec. 23, 2007, from http://nbcsports.msnbc.com/id/17982146/I/print/1/displaymode/1098/print/1/displaymode/1098/.

Broido, E. M. "Understanding Diversity in Millennial Students." In M. D. Coomes and R. DeBard (eds.), *Serving the Millennial Generation.* New Directions for Student Services, no. 106. San Francisco: Jossey-Bass, 2004.

Bush, G. W. "President Bush Discusses Michigan Affirmative Action Case." Jan. 15, 2003. Retrieved Mar. 23, 2008, from http://www.whitehouse.gov/news/releases/2003/01/20030115-7.html.

Carnevale, A. P., and Fry, R. A. *Crossing the Great Divide: Can We Achieve Equity When Generation Y Goes to College?* Princeton, N.J.: Educational Testing Service, 2000.

CNN.COM/US. "FBI: Hate Crimes Jump Nearly 8 Percent." Nov. 19, 2007. Retrieved Dec. 23, 2007, from http://www.cnn.com/2007/US/law/11/19/hate.crimes.ap/.

Crary, D. "U.S. Interracial Marriage Rate Soars." Apr. 12, 2007. Retrieved Dec. 23, 2007, from http://www.time.com/time/nation/article/0,8599,1609841,00.html.

Cruz, B. C., and Berson, M. J. "The American Melting Pot? Miscegenation Laws in the United States." *OAH Magazine of History*, 2001, *15*. Retrieved Dec. 23, 2007, from http://www.oah.org/pubs/magazine/family/cruz-berson.html.

Evans, N., Forney, D. S., and Guido-DiBrito, F. *Student Development in College: Theory, Research, and Practice.* San Francisco: Jossey-Bass, 1998.

Holmes, S. A. "Census Tests New Category to Identify Racial groups." *New York Times,* Dec. 6, 1996. Retrieved Dec. 23, 2007, from http://query.nytimes.com/gst/fullpage.html?res=9C07E5DB173FF935A35751C1A960958260&sec=&spon=&pagewanted=1.

Howe, N., and Strauss, W. *Millennials Rising: The Next Great Generation.* New York: Vintage Books, 2000.

Hurtado, S., and others. *Findings from the 2005 Administration of Your First College Year (YFC): National Aggregates.* Los Angeles: Higher Education Research Institute, 2007.

Jaschik, S. "An End to Picking One Box." *Inside Higher Ed,* Aug. 8, 2006. Retrieved Mar. 22, 2008, from http://www.insidehighered.com/news/2006/08/08/race.

Kassendorf, M., and Nasser, H. E. "Impact of Census' Race Data Debated." *USA Today,* Mar. 13, 2001. Retrieved Dec. 23, 2007, from http://www.usatoday.com/news/nation/census/2001-03-13-census-impact.htm.

King, M. L. "Dr. King's Presentation," Jan. 11, 1968. Retrieved Dec. 23, 2007, from http://www.onu.edu/library/onuhistory/king/king96.htm.

McCormick, A. C. "Swirling and Double-Dipping: New Patterns of Student Attendance and Their Implications for Higher Education." In J. E. King, E. L. Andersen, and M. E. Corrigan (eds.), *Changing Student Attendance Patterns: Challenges for Policy and Practice.* New Directions for Higher Education, no. 121. San Francisco: Jossey-Bass, 2003.

Millem, J. F., and Umbach, P. D. "The Influence of Precollege Factors on Students' Predispositions Regarding Diversity Activities in College." *Journal of College Student Development,* 2003, *44*, 611–624.

Nash, G. *Forbidden Love.* New York: Holt, 1999.

NPR. "Poll: African-Americans Pessimistic About Black Progress." *Tell Me More,* Nov. 14, 2007. Retrieved Dec. 23, 2007, from http://www.npr.org/templates/story/story.php?storyId=16284357&ft=1&f=1001.

Orfield, G., and Lee, C. "Historic Reversals, Accelerating Resegregation, and the Need for New Integration Strategies." Aug. 2007. Retrieved Dec. 23, 2007, from http://www.civilrightsproject.ucla.edu/research/deseg/reversals_reseg_need.pdf.

Pike, G. R., Kuh, G. D., and Gonyea, R. M. "Evaluating the Rationale for Affirmative Action in College Admissions: Direct and Indirect Relationships Between Campus Diversity and Gains in Understanding Diverse Groups." *Journal of College Student Development,* 2007, *48*, 166–182.

Pryor, J. H., and others. *The American Freshman: Forty Year Trends*. Los Angeles: Higher Education Research Institute, UCLA, 2007.

Rankin, S. R., and Reason, R. R. "Differing Perceptions: How Students of Color and White Students Perceive Campus Climate for Underrepresented Groups." *Journal of College Student Development*, 2005, 46, 43–61.

Root, M.P.P. *The Multiracial Experience: Racial Borders as the New Frontier*. Thousand Oaks, Calif.: Sage, 1996.

Smith, D. G., and others. *Diversity Works: The Emerging Picture of How Students Benefit*. Washington, D.C.: Association of American Colleges and Universities, 1997.

Smothers, R. "Principal Causes Furor on Mixed-Race Couples." Mar. 16, 1994. Retrieved Jan. 5, 2008, from http://query.nytimes.com/gst/fullpage.html?res=9E05E6D9113DF 935A25750C0A962958260&sec=&spon=&pagewanted=all.

Stein, N. "Affirmative action and the persistence of racism." *Social Justice*, 1995, 22(3). Retrieved March 22, 2008, from http://www.highbeam.com/doc/2G1-18285711.html.

Ziedenberg, J., and Schiraldi, V. "Cellblocks or Classrooms? The Funding of Higher Education and Corrections and Its Impact on African American Men." Sept. 18, 2002. Retrieved Dec. 23, 2007, from http://www.justicepolicy.org/images/upload/0209_REP_ CellblocksClassrooms_BB-AC.pdf.

PAUL SHANG is assistant vice chancellor for student development at the University of Missouri-Kansas City and a past president of ACPA—College Student Educators International.

NEW DIRECTIONS FOR STUDENT SERVICES • DOI: 10.1002/ss

2

This chapter presents an overview of theories that have been used to describe identity development of biracial and multiracial college students.

Research on Biracial and Multiracial Identity Development: Overview and Synthesis

Kristen A. Renn

Racial identity development among college students with parents from different heritage groups was largely unexplored until the 1990s, when two forces—one demographic, the other theoretical—converged to stimulate interest in understanding the experiences and identities of biracial and multiracial youth. The increasing number of students from two or more races (Renn, 2004) drew the attention of student affairs professionals just as student development researchers moved into a period of close study of individual identity groups (for example, Black, Asian American, gay/lesbian/bisexual). Although it might have occurred without this convergence, a body of research from the mid-1990s to the present has produced a solid foundation of theory to support student affairs practice regarding multiracial college students. In this chapter, I provide an overview and synthesis of this research; other chapters in this volume describe how student affairs professionals can use these theories.

A decade ago, student development scholars who tried to describe the experiences of biracial and multiracial youth turned to two models (Poston, 1990; Root, 1990). In 2008, the literature has broadened substantially to include psychological, sociological, and ecological models for understanding the identities of mixed-heritage college students (for example, Kilson, 2001; Renn, 2004; Rockquemore and Brunsma, 2002; Wallace, 2001, 2003; Wijeyesinghe, 2001). A move away from linear models mirroring predominant minority identity development models (Atkinson, Morten, and Sue,

NEW DIRECTIONS FOR STUDENT SERVICES, no. 123, Fall 2008   © Wiley Periodicals, Inc.
Published online in Wiley InterScience (www.interscience.wiley.com) • DOI: 10.1002/ss.282

1979; Cross, 1995; Helms, 1995) to ecological models (Renn, 2003, 2004; Root, 1998; Wijeyesinghe, 2001) that explain factors contributing to identity development characterizes the research. It is important to note that most studies of biracial college students rely on qualitative methods and limited samples; an exception is the survey research of Rockquemore and Brunsma (2002), which is limited instead by the decision to study only students of Black and White heritage. Most recently, psychologists (Bracey, Bamaca, and Umana-Taylor, 2004; Shih, Bonam, Sanchez, and Peck, 2007; Shih and Sanchez, 2005) have contributed substantively to understanding developmental and educational impacts related to holding a multiracial identity in adolescence and early adulthood.

Foundational Theories of Biracial Identity Development: Poston and Root

Poston (1990) and Root (1990) were the first scholars to publish models for the development of healthy biracial identity. Countering a history of skepticism about the possibility for healthy resolution of racial identity in biracial individuals, psychologists Poston and Root offered alternatives to past models that hypothesized a "marginal" (Stonequist, 1937) existence for biracial people. They based their proposals in part on clinical experience as counselors and, for Root, in part on personal experience.

Poston (1990) claimed that existing models of minority identity development (Cross, 1987; Morten and Atkinson, 1983) did not accurately reflect the experiences of biracial individuals and proposed a "new and positive model" (p. 153) with five levels:

1. *Personal identity.* Young children hold a personal identity that is not necessarily linked to a racial reference group.
2. *Choice of group categorization.* Based on personal factors (such as appearance and cultural knowledge) and factors defining perceived group status and social support, an individual chooses a multicultural existence that includes both parents' heritage groups or a dominant culture from one background.
3. *Enmeshment/denial.* Guilt at not being able to identify with all aspects of his or her heritage may lead to anger, shame, or self-hatred; resolving the guilt and anger is necessary to move beyond this level.
4. *Appreciation.* Individuals broaden their racial reference group through learning about all aspects of their backgrounds, though individuals may choose to identify with one group more than with others.
5. *Integration.* This level represents a multicultural existence in which the individual values all of her or his ethnic identities.

Poston acknowledged that this model resembled the earlier ones (Cross, 1987; Morten and Atkinson, 1983) that he rejected, but he accommodated the specificity of biracial experience by acknowledging the difference between monoracial and multiracial identities in the middle three levels of his model. Missing from Poston's model is Cross's and Morten and Atkinson's emphasis on societal racism as a factor in the lives of people of color, an element that later theorists would reintroduce. Also missing is the possibility of multiple healthy identity outcomes for the diversity of multiracial people, an exclusion that formed the basis of future inquiries by other researchers who observed an array of apparently healthy identities in biracial adults. Inclusion of personal and environmental factors in the second level (choice of group categorization) also foreshadowed the ecological perspective of later models of multiracial identity. Poston's model is particularly useful in understanding biracial identity development as compared to minority identity development models often used in student affairs work (Cross, 1995; Helms, 1995).

Root (1990) also allied her model with the early stages of minority identity development models (Atkinson, Morten, and Sue, 1979), altering their later stages to reflect the observation that when many biracial individuals with White heritage reach adolescence, they cannot fully reject majority culture and immerse themselves in a minority community, as minority identity development models typically posited. Citing societal racism and internalized oppression, Root posited that biracial teens—assuming that they are at least partly White—entered a period of turmoil and possibly a "dual existence" (p. 200) when they might appear popular but feel as though they do not fit into any social group. According to Root, dating and tokenism (that is, being asked to be the "minority representative") surface as issues with particular impact on biracial adolescents. Gender differences among mixed-race youth may exacerbate or alleviate the effects of racial discrimination.

Root (1990) proposed four potentially positive resolutions of the tensions of biracial identity:

1. *Acceptance of the identity society assigns.* Family and a strong alliance with and acceptance by a (usually minority) racial group provide support for identifying with the group into which others assume the biracial individual most belongs.
2. *Identification with both racial groups.* Depending on societal support and personal ability to maintain this identity in the face of potential resistance from others, the biracial individual may be able to identify with both (or all) heritage groups.
3. *Identification with a single racial group.* The individual chooses one group, independent of social pressure, to identify himself or herself in a particular way (as in resolution 1).
4. *Identification as a new racial group.* The individual may move fluidly among racial groups but identifies most strongly with other biracial people, regardless of specific heritage backgrounds.

Root (1990) accounted for the impact of racism on identity and intro-duced the possibility of a new identity group: biracial or multiracial. She also proposed that an individual might self-identify in more than one way at the same time or move fluidly among identities. Root's model opened the door for the emergence of empirically derived, nonlinear models of identity development in mixed-race students.

Ecology Models of Identity Development in Mixed-Race College Students

In the mid-1990s, as mixed-race students were becoming a more visible and vocal population and student development researchers were beginning to analyze specific aspects of identity (for example, Black identity, lesbian iden-tity, Catholic identity), the question of multiracial student experiences and identity captured a modest amount of attention. Two main concepts emerged from this period; the first presented patterns of identity observed among mixed-race students, and the second proposed ecological, social, and psychological contributors to the development of multiracial identities. It is important to note that these studies occurred against a backdrop of increasing access to Internet technologies that have become a key factor in multiracial research and social and political organizing, as by the non-profit political and social action group MAVIN Foundation, which has a substan-tial online organizing presence. Another key factor during this time was the 1997 decision by the U.S. Office of Management and Budget to change fed-eral data collection, including the 2000 U.S. Census, to offer for the first time the option for respondents to identify themselves in more than one racial category (see Chapter Ten, this volume).

Patterns of Identity Among Multiracial College Students.   In a grounded theory study of students from three postsecondary institutions, I (Renn, 2000) identified five patterns of identity among biracial and multi-racial college students. I later expanded the study geographically and elab-orated on the five patterns (Renn, 2004). Adopting the premise that college provides opportunities for identity exploration in academic, social, and peer involvement settings, this approach to multiracial identity takes a distinctly ecological perspective, as described in the next section. The five patterns I (Renn, 2000, 2004) identified were:

1. *Student holds a monoracial identity.* As in Root's third resolution (1990), the individual chooses one of his or her heritage backgrounds with which to identify.
2. *Student holds multiple monoracial identities, shifting according to the sit-uation.* Personal and contextual factors affect which of an individual's heritage groups he or she identifies with at a given time and place; this pattern is like Root's second resolution (1990).

3. *Student holds a multiracial identity.* The individual elects an identity that is neither one heritage nor another, but of a distinct "multiracial" group on par with other racial categories: Root's fourth resolution (1990).
4. *Student holds an extraracial identity by deconstructing race or opting out of identification with U.S. racial categories.* Not seen among Root's resolutions (1990), this pattern represents an individual's resistance to what he or she may see as artificial categories that have been socially constructed by the dominant, monoracial, White majority.
5. *Student holds a situational identity, identifying differently in different contexts.* Inherent in Root's resolutions (1990), situational identity describes a fluid identity pattern in which an individual's racial identity is stable, but different elements are more salient in some contexts than in others.

In a sample of fifty-six students from six institutions, I (Renn, 2004) found that nearly half (48 percent) identified themselves in each of the first two patterns, 89 percent held a distinctly multiracial identity, nearly one-quarter (23 percent) held an extraracial identity, and 61 percent identified themselves situationally (which explains why the total is more than 100 percent). When identity patterns were considered by students' gender, class year, institution, and heritage combinations, some differences were observed, but the tendency for students to identify themselves across patterns persisted throughout the data.

I (Renn, 2000, 2003, 2004) used a human ecological approach to understand multiracial identity, but important contributions to theory come also from sociology and educational psychology. Sociologist Marion Kilson (2001) studied young adults (college and noncollege) and reported identities similar to four of my five (Renn, 2004)—excluding the multiple monoracial identities category. Another pair of sociologists, Kerry Ann Rockquemore and David Brunsma (2002), surveyed 177 Black-White college students and reported four categories similar to Kilson's. Education psychologist Kendra Wallace (2001) studied 15 high school and college students and found evidence to confirm four of my (Renn, 2004) patterns, excluding the extraracial category. Although the studies all have limitations related to sample, the convergence of data strongly suggests that there are at least five ways that multiracial young people in college may identify themselves.

Factors Influencing Racial Identity Among Multiracial College Students. Smaller than the body of research on how multiracial students identify themselves is the literature on how they may come to have those identities. Evidence supports a person-environment or psychosocial process that is implicit in earlier models of racial identity development (Atkinson, Morten, and Sue, 1979; Cross, 1995; Helms, 1995). I (Renn, 2003, 2004) used an ecological approach, and it is possible to consider Charmaine Wijeyesinghe's factor model of multiracial identity (2001) and Wallace's work (2001, 2003) through this lens to examine factors that influence multiracial college students' identities. Of these ecological influences, three recurring themes in the literature are physical appearance, cultural knowledge, and peer culture.

Across several studies (Renn, 2004; Root, 2003; Wallace, 2003; Wijeyesinghe, 2001), how a multiracial individual looks—skin tone, hair texture and color, eye and nose shape, and so forth—strongly influences his or her identity. Whether a woman "looks Black enough" according to her peers to be part of a particular student organization, or whether a man is told that he looks "too Asian" to participate in a Latino cultural festival, students routinely confront messages that college campuses are places where authenticity is at stake in daily interactions, student organizations, and even the classroom. Professors and teaching assistants are not immune from societal stereotypes that link physical appearance to assumptions about cultural backgrounds, and mixed-race students report encountering ignorance, disbelief, and occasional outright hostility from instructors (Renn, 2004). Confirming Root's proposition (1990) that one option is to accept the identity that society assigns, multiracial students' identity choices may be constrained by how others interpret their appearance. They must also negotiate the campus racial landscape with an appearance that is not always recognizable to others, unwittingly provoking some discomfort until they can answer the *What [race] are you?* questions that they report as commonplace (Kilson, 2001; Renn, 2004; Wallace, 2001, 2003).

Cultural knowledge of their various heritage groups is a second major factor in mixed-race college students' identities (Renn, 2004; Wallace, 2003). Depending on knowledge learned from parents, family, and community prior to college, multiracial students may arrive on campus with extensive cultural knowledge of their diverse backgrounds, much knowledge on one or two backgrounds but limited or no knowledge of others, or limited knowledge of any particular heritage background. As with appearance, questions of authenticity, legitimacy, and fitting in arise in relation to cultural knowledge (Renn, 2000, 2004; Wallace, 2003). Students reported that speaking Spanish or an Asian language might be a passport into a community of students of color, as might listening to certain kinds of music or partaking of any one of dozens of ethnically marked elements of youth culture. Biracial students who had not learned about various aspects of their heritage before coming to college sometimes took courses, studied abroad, or participated in cocurricular activities aimed at learning more about their background (Renn, 2004). Armed with this knowledge, they might feel more confident to identify themselves with previously unexplored aspects of their identity; Poston (1990) proposed this "appreciation" level (level four in his model) in a general way, but college students have a number of resources close at hand to undertake this process. Considered in an ecological approach, appearance and cultural knowledge represent aspects of the individual, but the individual does not operate alone to influence identity development.

NEW DIRECTIONS FOR STUDENT SERVICES • DOI: 10.1002/ss

The context of college peer culture is a critical aspect of multiracial students' identity development. Wijeyesinghe (2001) identified social and historical context as factors in choice of racial identity. Participants in my studies and Wallace's cited the availability of a community of other biracial and multiracial students, a growing phenomenon that is discussed in Chapters Five and Six in this volume, as important supports for the development of separate multiracial identity. Resistance from monoracial students of color and racism among White students were additional aspects of peer culture that influenced their identities. I (Renn, 2000) found that the extent to which a campus peer culture supported or worked against students moving among identity groups was another important influence; at some campuses in this study, students moved easily among identity-based social groups, while at others, there was a clear delineation among groups, and membership in one precluded membership in another.

A full description of the operation of peer culture is beyond the scope of this chapter, but the influence of peers on student development and identity is well established (see Astin, 1984; Kaufman and Feldman, 2004), and it is not surprising that peers influence multiracial identity development as well. But as Poston (1990) and Root (1990) posited when contrasting their models to existing models of minority identity development, there are aspects of mixed-race experiences that make inadequate a simple application of existing theory to the experience of multiracial people. Considering not only the presence of various identity-based groups on campus but also the peer-supported ability to move among them is an example of how prevailing thinking about racial identity development and peers can be made more applicable to understanding multiracial college students.

Additional factors that have been linked to multiracial identity development in college students include gender, social class, family and family status, age, spirituality, social awareness and orientation, and geographical region (Renn, 2004; Rockquemore and Brunsma, 2002; Root, 1998, 2003; Shih, Bonam, Sanchez, and Peck, 2007, Wallace, 2003; Wijeyesinghe, 2001). Findings are not consistent across studies, but evidence suggests that personal and environmental factors combine to influence multiracial identity in college students.

Psychological Studies of Impact of Multiracial Identity

Written at the height of the pseudoscientific eugenics movement that aimed to improve the quality of the human gene pool, early literature on biracial individuals postulated poor mental and physical outcomes for these "marginal" people (Stonequist, 1937). More recent attention from researchers provides ample evidence that positive multiracial identity is linked to good psychological health. For example, multiracial adolescents' ability to identify themselves in categories that accurately represent their heritages and lived identity has been shown to promote higher self-esteem, a higher sense of efficacy, and lower stereotype vulnerability (Bracey, Bamaca, and Umana-Taylor, 2004; Shih, Bonam, Sanchez, and Peck, 2007; Shih and Sanchez, 2004). Although these studies are not limited to college student samples, it seems reasonable to apply their findings to traditional-age biracial college students who are in late adolescence. Extension of this research into older college populations will be a welcome addition to the literature.

Conclusion

These three bodies of research provide a foundation for understanding the experiences and identities of mixed-race students. They complement one another, yet must be understood within the limitations and strengths of each. Reliance on small samples of traditional-age students in qualitative studies (Kilson, 2001; Renn, 2004; Wallace, 2001) necessarily limits the transferability of findings to the national population of mixed-race students. Including participants from only one heritage combination (Rockquemore and Brunsma, 2002; Wijeyesinghe, 2001) introduces another kind of limitation. Relying on studies of precollege youth leaves gaps in knowledge about the identities, experiences, and psychological outcomes of multiracial college students. Yet as a whole, the body of research, combined with emerging literature such as that presented in this volume, provides a reasonably sound foundation for understanding and working with multiracial students in higher education.

References

Astin, A. W. "Student Involvement: A Development Theory for Higher Education." *Journal of College Student Personnel,* 1984, *25,* 297–308.
Atkinson, D., Morten, G., and Sue, D. W. *Counseling American Minorities: A Cross-Cultural Perspective.* Dubuque, Iowa: Brown Company, 1979.
Bracey, J. R., Bamaca, M. Y., and Umana-Taylor, A. J. "Examining Ethnic Identity and Self-Esteem Among Biracial and Monoracial Adolescents." *Journal of Youth and Adolescence,* 2004, *33,* 123–132.
Cross, W. E. "A Two-Factor Theory of Black Identity: Implications for the Study of Identity Development in Minority Children." In J. S. Phinney and M. J. Rotherham (eds.), *Children's Ethnic Socialization: Pluralism and Development.* Thousand Oaks, Calif.: Sage, 1987.
Cross, W. E., Jr. "The Psychology of Nigrescence: Revisiting the Cross Model." In J. G. Ponterotto, J. M. Casas, L. A. Suzuki, and C. M. Alexander (eds.), *Handbook of Multicultural Counseling.* Thousand Oaks, Calif.: Sage, 1995.
Helms, J. E. "An Update of Helms's White and People of Color Racial Identity Development Models." In J. G. Ponterotto, J. M. Casas, L. A. Suzuki, and C. M. Alexander (eds.), *Handbook of Multicultural Counseling.* Thousand Oaks, Calif.: Sage, 1995.
Kaufman, P., and Feldman, K. A. "Forming Identities in College: A Sociological Approach." *Research in Higher Education,* 2004, *45,* 463–496.
Kilson, M. *Claiming Place: Biracial Young Adults of the Post-Civil Rights Era.* Westport, Conn.: Bergin & Garvey, 2001.

Morten, G., and Atkinson, D. R. "Minority Identity Development and Preference for Counselor Race." *Journal of Negro Education*, 1983, *52*, 156–161.

Poston, W.S.C. "The Biracial Identity Development Model: A Needed Addition." *Journal of Counseling and Development*, 1990, *69*, 152–155.

Renn, K. A. "Patterns of Situational Identity Among Biracial and Multiracial College Students." *Review of Higher Education*, 2000, *23*, 399–420.

Renn, K. A. "Understanding the Identities of Mixed-Race College Students Through a Developmental Ecology Lens." *Journal of College Student Development*, 2003, *44*, 383–403.

Renn, K. A. *Mixed Race Students in College: The Ecology of Race, Identity, and Community.* Albany, N.Y.: SUNY Press, 2004.

Rockquemore, K. A., and Brunsma, D. L. *Beyond Black: Biracial Identity in America.* Thousand Oaks, Calif.: Sage, 2002.

Root, M.P.P. "Resolving 'Other' Status: Identity Development of Biracial Individuals." *Women and Therapy*, 1990, *9*, 185–205.

Root, M.P.P. "Experiences and Processes Affecting Racial Identity Development: Preliminary Results from the Biracial Sibling Project." *Cultural Diversity and Mental Health*, 1998, *4*, 237–247.

Root, M.P.P. "Racial Identity Development and Persons of Mixed Race Heritage." In M.P.P. Root and M. Kelley (eds.), *Multiracial Child Resource Book: Living Complex Identities.* Seattle, Wash.: MAVIN Foundation, 2003.

Shih, M., Bonam, C., Sanchez, D. T., and Peck, C. "The Social Construction of Race: Biracial Identity and Vulnerability to Stereotypes." *Cultural Diversity and Ethnic Minority Psychology*, 2007, *13*, 125–133.

Shih, M., and Sanchez, D. T. "Perspectives and Research on the Positive and Negative Implications of Having Multiple Racial Identities." *Psychological Bulletin*, 2005, *131*, 569–591.

Stonequist, E. V. *The Marginal Man: A Study in Personality and Culture Conflict.* New York: Russell & Russell, 1937.

Wallace, K. R. *Relative/Outsider: The Art and Politics of Identity Among Mixed Heritage Students.* Westport, Conn.: Ablex, 2001.

Wallace, K. R. "Contextual Factors Affecting Identity Among Mixed Heritage College Students." In M.P.P. Root and M. Kelley (eds.), *Multiracial Child Resource Book: Living Complex Identities.* Seattle, Wash.: MAVIN Foundation, 2003.

Wijeyesinghe, C. L. "Racial Identity in Multiracial People: An Alternative Paradigm." In C. L. Wijeyesinghe and B. W. Jackson III (eds.), *New Perspectives on Racial Identity Development: A Theoretical and Practical Anthology.* New York: New York University Press, 2001.

KRISTEN A. RENN is associate professor of higher, adult, and lifelong education at Michigan State University.

3

This chapter presents preliminary findings from a study of the experiences and self-labeling of ten individuals who are biracial and whose parents identify themselves as monoracial members of minority groups. Implications for student affairs educators are shared.

Exploring the Experiences and Self-Labeling of Mixed-Race Individuals with Two Minority Parents

Donna M. Talbot

As Renn (2003) and others have articulated clearly, the absurdity of studying race as if it were a fixed concept is surpassed by the necessity of understanding the experiences of individuals who identify themselves racially as mixed race or biracial. While researchers of multiracial students do not seek to validate a fixed, biological concept of race, we recognize the importance of validating the social construction and impact of race on students' experiences. According to Lee and Bean (2004, p. 221), "Currently, 1 in 40 persons identifies himself or herself as multiracial, and this figure is twice as high for those under the age of 18. By the year 2050, as many as 1 in 5 Americans could claim a multiracial background."

With increasing numbers of multiracial individuals and interracial relationships, the potential for rapid growth of this population on campus is unprecedented. Despite this emerging reality, the literature on mixed-race and multiracial persons is very limited, providing little guidance for student affairs educators. To address this need, I conducted a study of mixed-race individuals with two minority parents.

Background and Implementation of the Study

It is important and ethical that as the primary researcher, I recognize and attempt to understand the influence that personal and professional experiences have on my decisions while conducting the study and analyzing the

NEW DIRECTIONS FOR STUDENT SERVICES, no. 123, Fall 2008 © Wiley Periodicals, Inc.
Published online in Wiley InterScience (www.interscience.wiley.com) • DOI: 10.1002/ss.283

data collected. My experiences as a mixed-race (Japanese, French Canadian, Native American) student affairs professional and educator are what drive this research. Having responded to the question, "What are you?" (too many times to count), having been told, "Of course, you're good at statistics" (because I am Asian), and having "passed as White" all within a few hours of each other, I am acutely aware of the challenges of being a mixed-race person in higher education in a highly racialized country. Yet as challenging as my experiences have been, I cannot help but believe that those experiences are uniquely different for individuals who are mixed race with no dominant heritage, with no ability to "pass" as White. This belief is fueled by my continued experiences and study of power and privilege as they relate to race.

In 1999 when this study was conceived, research on mixed-race folks was nearly nonexistent and included primarily individuals who had at least one parent who was White (see Root, 1996). I could locate no studies that focused solely or primarily on biracial or multiracial individuals who had two racial minority parents. Given the nature of White racial superiority in the United States (Lee and Bean, 2004) and the importance of hearing voices of all who contribute to society, the need to engage individuals who experience being mixed race without any dominant group status, without having any known White heritage, was imperative.

Research Methods

The overall goal of the study was to explore the experiences of biracial individuals (with two parents from racial minority groups) coming to terms with selecting a racial label that felt comfortable (self-labeling) and the factors that influenced that process of self-labeling. Individuals were asked to reflect on their process of self-labeling over time, from childhood to adulthood. Additional questions sought to understand the influences of the larger society, the cultural communities in which participants were raised, cultural traditions celebrated by their families, and challenges they faced.

Sampling and Sample. The study involved electronic interviews with ten people from across the United States. The protocol for the study stipulated that participants label themselves as biracial and have "monoracial ethnic minority" biological parents from two different ethnic/racial groups as identified by the U.S. Census categories (at the time defined as Black/African American, Asian, Latino/Hispanic, and Indian/Native American). Influenced by my professional training and beliefs about the effects of college on students (as explicated by student development and identity formation theories; see Evans, Forney, and Guido-DiBrito, 1998), participants in the study must have completed at least two years of college. The participants also had to have grown up in the United States; this condition was based on a fundamental assumption emphasized in this volume (see Chapters One and Nine, this volume) that concepts of race and culture are shaped by the sociopolitical issues within a country (see also Root, 1996).

I contacted individuals through minority-focused listservs affiliated with higher education and invited them to participate. After receiving human subjects board approval, I posted a general invitation with my contact information, as well as a request to forward the invitation to other relevant listservs and individuals. Announcing the study and requesting participation through electronic listservs was an intentional sampling technique seeking to draw the broadest possible range of biracial participants. When an individual contacted me, I conducted a short screening interview by telephone to determine if the respondent was biracial (not biethnic, that is, having parents from different ethnic groups within one racial category, such as Chinese and Korean), with only two minority racial heritages. To determine eligibility, I asked about the racial categorization of parents, grandparents, and great-grandparents.

After screening almost forty people, I identified ten individuals who fit the protocol: four men and six women, ranging from twenty to thirty-four years old and averaging about twenty-six years of age. As the protocol stipulated, participants had a minimum of two years of college and had been raised in the United States; most of the participants had graduated from college, and a few had master's degrees. Several of the participants had at least one parent who was not born in the United States. Participants resided in all geographical regions of the United States except the Southeast, and they represented a variety of ethnic/racial backgrounds: Japanese, Korean, Chinese, African American, Jamaican, Mexican American, Puerto Rican, South American, and Native American. Five were Asian and Black/African American; three Asian and Hispanic/Latino; one Hispanic/Latino and Black/African American; and one Native American and Black/African American.

Data Collection.   Participants were given a choice of a phone or e-mail interview (see James and Busher, 2006, on online interviewing). Despite the acknowledgment that e-mail is not a guaranteed confidential medium, everyone selected the e-mail interview because it gave them time to reflect on the questions and the freedom to respond according to their own schedules (James and Busher, 2006). The research team also discussed the likelihood that participants in this study, like many students in colleges and universities currently, were as comfortable communicating electronically as by speaking.

Each participant received three sets of questions, one set at a time. After a participant completed and returned one set, we reviewed the responses and generated follow-up questions for clarification or to elicit stories that elaborated on a point. As the research progressed, we addressed thoughts and language from earlier interviews. Completion of one set of questions, including follow-up questions, triggered another. This process continued until all three sets and follow-up questions were completed and individuals had an opportunity to share any other reflections or comments. When all the interviews were completed, they were compiled, printed, and distributed to the research team for review and analysis.

The research team acknowledged that conducting the interviews by e-mail could have influenced the depth of the interchanges about participants' experiences. While the participants seemed comfortable and adept at electronic conversations, the researchers (all of whom had training as counselors) were less so. Because of this potential limitation, we took a very conservative stance on data analysis and breadth of findings. Nevertheless, as one of the first studies focused on mixed-race individuals with no White heritage, the interviews provide preliminary insights into participants' experiences.

Data Analysis. After each participant completed a set of questions, we reviewed the responses or potential follow-up questions and culled the responses for language to begin forming initial categories of themes. Once all the interviews were completed, each member of the research team read a completed set of questions and follow-up questions for each of the ten participants. Throughout these readings, we took notes on language that the participants used to describe themselves racially and their racial experiences; we also noted factors that influenced how participants labeled themselves racially. After carefully reading all interviews, we generated initial categories or themes across the ten interviews to discuss coding the data within and across participants' responses (Kvale, 1996). Through a process of compiling language and quotations used by participants in the e-mail interviews, we synthesized three broad categories from the data. Longer interviews with more participants are necessary to provide dimension and details within these three categories.

Results

Three broad categories surfaced in all ten interviews: families and communication (or lack thereof), the omnipresence of phenotype, and the process of self-labeling. I interpret and present these findings with the goal of providing some support to mixed-race individuals in colleges and universities.

Families and Communication (or Lack Thereof). In his chapter on communication about race in interracial families, Orbe (1999) discussed four orientations exhibited in Black-White families. Like most other research that focuses on the mixed-race experience, overtones of privilege and White superiority within the family of origin guided Orbe's findings. Initially I assumed that power and privilege would not be relevant for the participants in this study since no one within the family unit had White heritage or lineage. Although issues of race and being a racial minority were always present within the family (for example, participants' families ate food from their cultures, attended cultural events and festivities, and immersed themselves in families and communities that represented each parent's heritage) and largely embraced by parents, race was rarely discussed openly. Participants reported that despite this implied acknowledgment of race and culture, explicit discussions or communication about race, especially being biracial, were nonexistent between parents and children.

While reflecting on this factor, research team members wondered if both parents' everyday experiences were so embedded in race that having conversations about their racial experiences seemed redundant. In contrast to this experience, two participants recalled one or two occasions when their parents indicated that they, the participants, were special because of who they were or that they were lucky because they had exposure to two distinct cultures. Since all of the participants' parents, as well as their grandparents, identified monoracially, they may not have understood the difference and importance of being biracial. Within the family, any discussions or arguments focused on the mixed-race experience were shared by siblings.

The Omnipresence of Phenotype. References to the power of phenotype (physical appearance and features) were pervasive during the interviews (see also Chapters Two and Four, this volume). When asked about how society perceived them, all participants discussed their physical appearance, especially skin color. This was particularly true for individuals who were half Black/African American. From an early age, all participants could place themselves along a continuum of skin color, hair texture, eye shape, and facial structure. No matter how they identified themselves internally or to others, participants were still labeled by their physical appearance. This constant external labeling came from family, close friends, teachers and other faculty, random strangers, and student affairs professionals in colleges and universities. Participants wrote that they believed the individuals doing the labeling were not aware of their actions. For example, one individual wrote about participating in a multicultural educational program; the administrator running the program told the participant, who identifies as Asian–African American, to go with the Black students since she "looked mostly Black." The participant felt frustrated and hopeless since she perceived this to be an unconscious and uninformed response from someone who works in multicultural education and should, according to the student, know better.

When asked about their families and siblings, participants first pointed out how their physical appearances aligned with one parent or the other. As Root (1996) noted, siblings can have, and as reported by participants in this study did have, very different physical appearances. The second component participants addressed was how each sibling's personality compared to what seemed to be stereotypical behaviors associated with a racial group. One Asian–African American woman described herself as having more physical attributes of someone who is Black (darker skin, tightly curled hair) but more personality characteristics stereotypically Asian (quiet, deferring to others), while her sister was petite with long dark hair and lighter skin but "acted more [stereotypically] Black" (outspoken, into hip-hop music).

Despite most of the participants' ability to move beyond traditional monoracial ways of thinking about and compartmentalizing race (as evidenced by self-labeling as biracial), when asked to describe themselves and their families, participants used the same racialized tools that society as a whole uses. They used descriptions of stereotypical behavior associated with race (talking Black, having good rhythm, being quiet and reserved) and physical attributes associated with race (kinky hair, flat nose, slanted eyes). As the research team mulled over the implications of this interpretation, we

NEW DIRECTIONS FOR STUDENT SERVICES • DOI: 10.1002/ss

were struck by how much our current language and terms drive how we talk and think about race. Perhaps, even though the participants were ready psychologically to engage race more complexly, they did not yet have a body of language to express that complexity.

The Process of Self-Labeling. During these electronic interviews, it was clear that coming to identify oneself as biracial was a process that evolved over time. As participants reflected on the racial labels they internalized, those labels changed from childhood to adolescence to adulthood. For some participants, self-identity (an internalized sense of who they are as racial beings) and self-labeling (becoming comfortable with a label they could share with an external world) were different processes. While all participants voiced the importance of embracing the two racial heritages of their parents, getting to that point differed for each person.

Participants who were half Black/African American struggled most against the strong messages of others, of society at large, about the label they should use to describe themselves. Some individuals began to question their allegiance to racial communities that represented their heritage when they were not openly accepted by those communities. Several individuals discussed the phenomenon of "not being enough" (not Black enough, not Latina enough, not Asian enough). Some participants seemed angry (as demonstrated by a different pattern of writing, for example typing in all capital letters) about this behavior from other racial minorities, although they never articulated this explicitly; after all, according to participants, these are folks who also experienced alienation on a regular basis because they were racial minorities. The participants implied that they felt more prepared for discrimination from Whites, the dominant group, than from members of their own groups.

Another challenge with coming to terms with self-identity and self-labeling related to negotiating uncharted waters or having no role models. Pointing to the importance of public role models, participants noted the impact on them of golfer Tiger Woods's public declaration that he was "Cablinasian" (a term he made up to describe his heritage: Caucasian, Black, American-Indian, and Asian). Other events having a similar impact included meeting a mixed-race individual or finding a mixed-race group on campus. In essence, having a well-respected athlete proudly declare his mixed-race heritage or interacting with others who embraced their multiracial backgrounds gave participants permission to do the same. Like Woods, three of the participants created their own racial self-labels: a Chicana and Japanese woman called herself "Chicanese"; a participant who is Asian and African American called herself "Triple A"; and "Korack" was the term chosen by a woman who is Korean and Black. For one young man, his self-label, though controversial to some, was connected to his love for his grandfather, who affectionately referred to him as his "Nigganese" (Black and Chinese) grandson; his grandfather was one of the few people in his family who openly recognized and addressed his biracial heritage. These self-made labels were empowering to the individuals who created and used them when asked rudely the standard question directed toward mixed-race folks: "What are you?"

When specifically asked how they came to understand or have knowledge about their two cultural heritages, most participants talked about the significant role of grandparents, college and university courses, books, and cultural celebrations or programming (for more on this phenomenon, see Chapters Two and Four, this volume). Again, while most recognized from an early age that they had two distinct racial heritages, embracing a label and having the language to discuss who they were was solidified in late adolescence or early adulthood, during college.

Implications of the Results

Several years have passed since this study was initiated. I use the term *initiated* rather than *conducted* because for me, this research is not complete; it represents a jumping-off point. In addition, since time does not stand still and the sociopolitical issues within the country continue to change, responses and reactions to mixed-race issues also continue to evolve. In the past decade, there have been major developments in the United States that influence the impact of the research findings. First, the 2000 U.S. Census has been released, studied, and interpreted from multiple angles (see Perlmann and Waters, 2002). That census marked the first time that individuals were allowed to check more than one box. While there are disputes about how many individuals actually exercised their right to identify as mixed race, the fact remains that the existence of multiracial individuals in this nation is now a matter of formal reporting structures recognized by the U.S. government (see Chapter Ten, this volume, for more on the policy change and higher education). Second, beginning in 1997 with the public introduction of Tiger Woods as "Cablinasian," the United States, in fact the entire world, has been bombarded with mixed-race or multiracial images by the media. The nomination of Barack Obama, who is of mixed white and African heritage, as Democractic presidential nominee in 2008 further raised the visibility of biracial Americans. Implications for the findings are shared against the backdrop of these three major events.

Student affairs professionals and like-minded educators recognize that college represents a time of holistic development for many students (Evans, Forney, and Guido-DiBrito, 1998). In the light of this belief, many professionals cannot comprehend students, especially racial minority students, who do not seem to understand something so basic to their everyday experiences as their race. But as the study participants highlighted, conversations and education about being mixed-race minorities can be rare, even within the family unit. In addition, individuals can be pressured to align with only one racial minority group (Renn, 2003; Root, 1996). Participants in this study struggled to find words to describe their experiences as mixed-race beings in a monoracial world. Even their families did not prepare them for this challenge. So it should not be surprising when mixed-race students do not come to college with racial identities fully formed and ready to articulate.

As professionals committed to developing the whole student, student affairs educators need to provide opportunities for racial exploration, as well as review institutional policies and procedures that may reinforce a monoracial perspective. All of the participants in the study reported that seeing or interacting with other mixed-race individuals was significant in their ability to positively self-identify and self-label. As challenging as it may be for monoracially identified minority students to find appropriate role models on campus, it is even more difficult for mixed-race students (see Chapter Four, this volume).

The biracial individuals in this study also reported that opportunities to be involved in race-based groups or activities that do not require them to "choose one [race]" helped them to feel whole. Especially in multicultural programming, it is important to be vigilant about how we have been taught to see the world through a monoracial lens. This awareness is critical since many mixed-race students in our study turned to multicultural offices for support and felt more frustrated and disheartened when they met ignorance. Education and exploration must be conducted with race-specific student organizations on campus about how to include and assist mixed-race students. As our participants pointed out, just because a student belongs to both the Black Student Union and the Asian Pacific American Network does not mean that he or she is not invested in both or should have to choose one to establish commitment.

Based on our study, the most difficult challenge seems to be helping individuals who identify themselves as monoracial understand the importance and power of "border crossings" (Root, 1996) for individuals who are mixed race. In an effort to provide role models and outlets for mixed-race students, one situation is to have a mixed-race student group that facilitates dialogue and education on campus (see Chapters Five and Six, this volume); this group can, for example, help sponsor speakers (for example, faculty, administrators, or public figures) who publicly identify themselves as mixed race. The facilitator for these dialogues and programs must be able to engage in and promote complex conversations about differences among mixed-race students. The goal is not to splinter an already small and tenuous group in colleges and universities, but to validate the depth and complex nature of race and racial experiences on campus.

Finally, for everyone, developing identity is a complicated process (Evans, Forney, and Guido-DiBrito, 1998). For mixed-race minority individuals, this process becomes even more challenging when there is limited language available to define their experiences and when others reveal discomfort with what they perceive as racial ambiguity. This discomfort is often imposed on mixed-race individuals by demanding that they use a standard or familiar racial label. Indeed, a number of student development theories and models define ambiguity or fluidity in identity as unfinished business or pathology (Evans, Forney, and Guido-DiBrito, 1998). One way to support the development of mixed-race students is to allow them to engage in their process free from predetermined racial identity and developmental labels. We can facilitate these students' development by creating spaces in higher education that encourage open discussion and debate a more realistic and flexible notion of race.

As Renn wrote in Chapter Two of this volume, professionals in higher education may need to move away from stage-based models that cannot, by their nature, incorporate the complexity of mixed-race experiences. We need to move from a monoracial perspective of the world to one that fully integrates mixed-race experiences as described in part by participants in the study reviewed in this chapter.

References

Evans, N. J., Forney, D. S., and Guido-DiBrito, F. *Student Development in College: Theory, Research, and Practice.* San Francisco: Jossey-Bass, 1998.

James, N., and Busher, H. "Credibility, Authenticity and Voice: Dilemmas in Online Interviewing." *Qualitative Research,* 2006, 6, 403–420.

Kvale, S. *InterViews: An Introduction to Qualitative Research Interviewing.* Thousand Oaks, Calif.: Sage, 1996.

Lee, J., and Bean, F. D. "America's Changing Color Lines: Immigration, Race/Ethnicity and Multiracial Identification." *Annual Review of Sociology,* 2004, 30, 221–242.

Orbe, M. P. "Communicating About 'Race' in Interracial Families." In T. J. Socha and R. C. Diggs (eds.), *Communication, Race, and Family: Exploring Communication in Black, White, and Biracial Families.* Mahwah, N.J.: Erlbaum, 1999.

Perlmann, J., and Waters, M. C. (eds.). *The New Race Question: How the Census Counts Multiracial Individuals.* New York: Russell Sage Foundation, 2002.

Renn, K. A. "Understanding the Identities of Mixed-Race College Students Through a Developmental Ecology Lens." *Journal of College Student Development,* 2003, 44, 383–403.

Root, M. *The Multiracial Experience: Racial Borders as the New Frontier.* Thousand Oaks, Calif.: Sage, 1996.

Donna M. Talbot is a professor of educational leadership and faculty coordinator of the Higher Education and Student Affairs Leadership program in the Department of Educational Leadership, Research, and Technology at Western Michigan University.

4

This chapter describes the perspectives and experiences of multiracial college students and offers recommendations for institutions of higher education to better support college students who identify as multiracial.

Student Perspectives on Multiracial Identity

Alissa R. King

When the U.S. 2000 Census allowed individuals to identify themselves in two or more racial categories, approximately 6.8 million people identified with more than one race (Jones and Smith, 2001). Interest in racial identity development among college students had just broken the surface in the 1990s (see Chapter Two, this volume), and following the 2000 census, even more attention was paid to the complexity of understanding multiracial identity (Cortés, 2000; DaCosta, 2003; Kenney, 2002; Miville, Constantine, Baysden, and So-Lloyd, 2005).

Recognizing the increasing diversity on college campuses (El-Khawas, 2003; Torres, 2007), coupled with an interest in the identity development of multiracial students (King, 2008; Renn, 2000, 2003, 2004), I illuminate the experiences of multiracial college students by using excerpts from my doctoral dissertation and examples from other sources that focus on multiracial college students (Brown, 2001; Gaskins, 1999; Israel, 2004; Miville, Constantine, Baysden, and So-Lloyd, 2005; Renn, 2000, 2003, 2004). I use personal narrative as a student who identifies as multiracial to further illustrate the experience of attending college. I organize these ideas according to challenges that multiracial students experience in navigating identity-based social and cultural spaces on campus (King, 2008; Renn, 2000). I also offer recommendations for college and university educators and leaders attempting to better support multiracial students.

Josselson (1996) stated, "Identity is the ultimate act of creativity. . . . [It] represents knowing who we are in the context of all that we might be

New Directions for Student Services, no. 123, Fall 2008 © Wiley Periodicals, Inc.
Published online in Wiley InterScience (www.interscience.wiley.com) • DOI: 10.1002/ss.284

. . . [and it] is what we make of ourselves within a society that is making something of us" (pp. 27–28). College encourages identity development in students by offering a dynamic environment where they can explore who they are (Chickering and Reisser, 1993; Sanford, 1966). Yet at the same time, others in the college environment are "making something of [them]" (Josselson, 1996, p. 28) and their identities. Identity development is thus not an isolated activity; it occurs through and because of interactions with others.

One of the dominant themes in Renn's study (2000, 2004) and my study (King, 2008) was the expressed need for physical, social, and psychological spaces for biracial and multiracial identity development. For Renn's participants, public spaces included "residence halls, student organizations, classrooms, and social events" (p. 405). The participants in my study spoke about public spaces such as student organizations specifically for biracial or multiracial students, or other organizations that were supportive of multiracial identity, and student social events pertaining to race. These public spaces provided access to like-minded and sometimes like-appearing or like-experienced others with whom the students could interact. These factors contributed heavily to multiracial students' racial identity development process.

Renn (2000) described private spaces as spaces where students could "[sort] through meanings of peer culture, family background, and personally held notions of culture, race, and self" (p. 405). Private spaces were accessed "through journal writing, academic projects, or conversations with trusted others" (p. 405). Private spaces for participants in my study came from having the opportunity to talk with supportive and open-minded others about challenges and celebrations related to identity and from having the opportunity to explore more about themselves in research projects in college classes.

Challenge to Navigating Campus Spaces: Physical Appearance

Two key challenges in navigating social and physical spaces in the college environment derive from how others perceive multiracial students' racial identities based on physical appearance and conformity to expected displays of cultural knowledge and ways of acting (Hall, 1996, 2004; King, 2008; Renn, 2003). These challenges then may provoke developmental outcomes (Brown, 2001; Kellogg, 2006; Renn, 2003). For participants in Brown's study (2001), college "catapulted some [of them] into a racial identity crisis" (p. 91) rather than relieving them from it. In Gaskins's book (1999), multiracial students shared their experiences. India, a multiracial Native American woman, provided an example of being asked about her racial identity: "I was eating dinner in the dorm. . . . One of the guys I knew came up . . . and said, 'India, what *are* you?'. . . I get asked what I am a lot. I usually just answer that I am mixed. But then that isn't enough of an answer for most people" (pp. 22–23).

Jayla, a participant in my study who is one-quarter Mexican and three-quarters White, went to college on a minority scholarship and described her experiences at an overnight retreat for other scholarship recipients: "I had to attend a class for the scholarship and then go to an overnight retreat with all the people in the scholarship. When I was on the retreat people kept coming up to me and being like, 'So what are you?' I had to learn how to answer that question."

Similarly, Israel (2004), a Chinese American–Jewish American, reflected on her time in college when others challenged the legitimacy of her racial identity:

In Charlottesville, people asked the question, "What are you?" I would tell people I'm half-Chinese and half-Jewish, and they seemed to accept that. The urban Ivy League students with whom I went to college were more critical. "You can't be half-Chinese and half-Jewish," they would say. . . . I never quite knew how to respond to this. It was years later that I finally realized that, since this was *my* identity, I got to decide how I wanted to describe it [p. 175].

Expressing the complexity of multiracial identity and the frequent invisibility of members of the racial group, a participant in a study by Miville, Constantine, Baysden, and So-Lloyd (2005) stated, "I think the big issue for multiracials, like me, is the fact that we are an ethnicity. . . . People forget about us in the whole minority spectrum" (p. 511). Yet another example of being forgotten or invisible is provided by Jasmine, a participant in my study whose multiracial identity is made up of Black, Cherokee, French, and Spanish heritages:

Most people don't think that I'm multiracial at all, they're like, "Oh, she's the black girl." I've noticed that people have difficulty describing people and I'm pretty sure that's usually the thing that clicks in someone's mind. They're like "Oh, do you know Jasmine? Yeah, she's the black one."

Another example of invisibility is illustrated by Fred:

I think it's a little different because some people don't even realize that I'm half-Japanese. Actually, one of my good friends for a year or two just found out last semester. He was talking to my friend and they were talking about it, and they actually made a bet about me. He didn't believe it, he was talking to my roommate, and he was surprised [Renn, 2004, p. 110].

In 1998, when I was a college freshman, I also encountered curiosity about my racial identity. As a participant in a minority program for new college students, I was frequently questioned about my racial legitimacy and asked, "What are you?" As a light-skinned multiracial woman with a racially ambiguous appearance and no knowledge of what my actual racial identity is because I am adopted, I was often miscategorized and, like Jasmine, lumped into categories based on my appearance, people assumed, I was (Latina, Middle Eastern, Brazilian, and others).

Challenge to Navigating Campus Spaces: Cultural Groups and Knowledge

A second key challenge to fitting in on campus that is frequently reported by biracial and multiracial students relates to the ways in which other students see them as fitting into monoracial cultural groups (King, 2008; Renn, 2000, 2004). The transition from high school to college, "a major life change [which] may be a source of strain [as] academic demands increase and new social relations are established" (Friedlander, Reid, Shupak, and Cribbie, 2007, p. 259), sometimes provokes culture-related identity questions among multiracial students. The search for new social relationships and supportive spaces can provide feelings of alienation and loneliness or feelings of acceptance and belonging (Daniel, 1996; Renn, 2000, 2003, 2004; Root, 1990). A first-year college student in Brown's study (2001) explained:

> Coming to college was one of the most important experiences in terms of my racial identity. All of a sudden I was faced with, You are black; you will join this organization. I started to get all the literature of the black alliances and all of a sudden it became a big issue, like What are you? Who are you going to hang with? Although it's okay to have a few white friends there is [are] limits to what is okay. I was really angry when I came here. I was like, Who the hell are you to judge me? That is why I am really excited about the biracial group [pp. 91–92].

Roxanne, another contributor to Gaskins's anthology (1999), felt lonely during her first year of college as she tried to fit in with a bicultural background. Navigating the college environment during a time when everyone was adjusting and having the added weight of her bicultural identity prompted her feelings of isolation. In Renn's study of multiracial college students (2000), Marisa shared, "I never really felt like I completely belong[ed]" (p. 409).

Even when physical and social spaces for people of color are available, personal appearance and lack of cultural knowledge affect multiracial college students' ability to be accepted by other students in those spaces. Scarlet, a participant in my study who is a Hawaiian and white multiracial student and described herself as "white-appearing," felt very uncomfortable in "students of color spaces" on her college campus. She explained,

> I identify more strongly as a person of color than I do as a white person and so it's frustrating because I don't feel comfortable going to students of color spaces because I'm not perceived as a student of color. I'm starting to be a lot more vocal about my intersecting identities and feeling uncomfortable in places where [there are] students of color.

NEW DIRECTIONS FOR STUDENT SERVICES • DOI: 10.1002/ss

Kira, a participant in Renn's study (2000), described what it was like trying to navigate spaces without being visually identifiable in terms of race or having the cultural markers that would legitimize her ability to fit into those spaces:

Because I don't have any easily identifiable Filipino traits, such as speaking a Filipino dialect, eating Filipino food at home, or even simply having a Filipino name, I often feel unsure that I share in [a common] Filipino experience, and I think that others in the group are feeling the same uncertainty about me [Renn, 2000, p. 393].

A student in Brown's study (2001) said, "The college situation was very confusing to me. My black friends demanded that I act black and my white friends wanted me to act white. I didn't know how to act anymore" (p. 92). Diaz (Gaskins, 1999) said, "When I was in school, I just knew that I was different. First of all, I never felt completely accepted by either group, blacks or Hispanics. My hair was different" (p. 57). Randolph (Gaskins, 1999) described how appearance hindered her ability to fit in: "One of the things I learned at Cornell is that you almost have to choose who you are. . . . Obviously if you look at me, I'm dark. I guess you'd relate to me as a black person. But I'm not black. For most of the black people at Cornell, I am a little too light" (pp. 90–91).

The examples here illustrate how appearance and lack of cultural nuances accentuated students' difference and made it difficult for them to fit into the racial and ethnic spaces on the college campus. According to Turner (1982) and Lickel and others (2000), having shared characteristics or similar traits is important for inclusion.

Jasmine, a participant in my study, also described an experience where she felt that she did not belong:

There was a time where they had a Native American weekend thing and one of my friends was like, "Oh, come with me." She's Navajo and because I'm one-eighth Cherokee, she was like, "Oh, you should come with me. I think it'll be fun." When I was there it was really awkward cuz I'm like, "I don't look like I have any Native American in me and these people are going to be like, *What are you doing here?*" I ended up leaving because I felt so uncomfortable.

In my college experience, I was often spoken to in Spanish by individuals who mistakenly thought I could speak it. I speak only English fluently, so that caused several awkward encounters where, in some cases, the person speaking to me got upset by believing I was choosing not to speak to them, when in reality, I simply could not.

Although I identified as biracial or multiracial, I felt at a disadvantage in certain social settings because I did not have what I felt were the adequate resources to blend in with my peers of color, such as language, cultural experiences, or cultural knowledge, to be a legitimate member of the group. I also perceived exclusion from the Black Student Alliance on my campus when I attended a meeting. When I entered the room, all eyes were on me. I was the lightest-skinned person there, and I immediately felt as if I did not belong. I never went to another meeting.

Fitting In: Finding Inclusive Social and Cultural Spaces on Campus

Although multiracial students in several studies (Brown, 2001; King, 2008; Renn, 2004) reported feeling invisible in or excluded from groups of students of color on campus, there were also times when students felt included in social and cultural groups of monoracial students of color. These experiences supported students' exploration of racial and cultural identity and feelings of fitting in on campus. A participant in Brown's study (2001) illustrated the relief she felt by finding an inclusive space:

> It was not until I got to . . . university that I was able to say that I am black without feeling that I was somehow cutting off or ignoring the white side of me. During pre-orientation as a freshman for the first time in my life I met a huge group of people, all minorities. Oh, it was the greatest feeling! I am not alone [p. 91].

Talisa, a Black and Mexican multiracial participant in my study, described her feelings about her college campus: "The great thing about being in the [support and networking program] is that I got so many things [of] what they try to do here. It's such a huge campus with so many people . . . and there are different ethnic and multicultural groups."

Allyse, a Mexican and Spanish participant in my study, praised her college for providing a comfortable school: "Walking around campus, I feel like everyone is there in support of everyone else. I don't feel like there's chastising or criticism or condescension." Finally, Joan, a White and Native American participant in my study, said this of her college campus: "I haven't utilized many of the racial identity resources [on campus], but I know they're there and I know there are people there if I choose to find them. There's so much of a support system and support groups. I feel very comfortable there."

These examples of student experiences illustrate some of the challenges and support that multiracial students encounter on a college campus. Some of the challenges include feeling pulled between various students-of-color organizations, feeling invisible, being bombarded with questions about racial identity, and feeling as if they do not have the cultural tools to appropriately navigate students-of-color spaces. Some of the support occurred when multiracial students found similar others with whom they could identify themselves and supportive spaces where they could explore their identity and gain a sense of belonging.

NEW DIRECTIONS FOR STUDENT SERVICES • DOI: 10.1002/ss

Recommendations: Creating Space

Multiracial individuals, especially those in the college setting, must continually define and redefine themselves in order to fit in (Renn, 2003). Finding a racial home helped multiracial students explore and make peace with who they are (Brown, 2001; King, 2008; Renn, 2000, 2003, 2004). It is therefore important for student affairs professionals to consider ways that their institutions can help multiracial students adjust and develop by offering spaces where these students can feel comfortable.

In reflecting on my college experience, for example, there were few physical spaces where I felt comfortable, but I did have many occasions within the classroom to explore my identities and talk with other students who also identified as multiracial. The university from which I graduated now has a student organization for biracial and multiracial students, several multicultural programs that include biracial and multiracial students, and a multicultural learning community that brings students of color together to talk about issues of race and ethnicity in Iowa and across the rest of the United States (Multicultural Student Affairs, 2007). These are exciting additions to the college campus that I wish had been available when I was a student there.

Recommendations for faculty include engaging faculty and staff in conversations about the invisibility of multiracial identity and encouraging faculty to include multiracial identity in their discussions about race and ethnicity in the classroom. Leaving these identities out further alienates students who claim a multiracial identity. (Kellogg and Niskodé provide additional recommendations in Chapter Ten, this volume.)

Recommendations for administrators include recruiting and hiring faculty who identify as multiracial so that multiracial students have visible mentors and role models to whom they might relate. This recommendation was similar to a finding in Renn's study (2004) in which the importance of visible like-others was supported: "Supporting mixed [race] faculty and staff in any efforts they might make to 'come out' as multiracial would be an important step toward increasing the visibility of mixed people in higher education" (p. 248). Overall, visibility, awareness, openness, and support are all strides that institutions of higher education should make toward creating a more inclusive campus environment for students who identify as multiracial.

Conclusion

In this chapter, I have shared some of the barriers to visibility and inclusion for multiracial students, emphasized the importance of creating physical and psychological spaces for multiracial students on the college campus where they can explore their identity, and highlighted some considerations for college communities to help multiracial students network, build community, feel as though they belong, and feel supported (Cortés, 2000; Renn, 2004; Sanford, 1966). More comprehensive recommendations are highlighted throughout this volume to prepare institutions of higher education for the expanding multiracial student population.

References

Brown, U. M. *The Interracial Experience: Growing Up Black/White Racially Mixed in the United States.* Westport, Conn.: Praeger, 2001.

Chickering, A. W., and Reisser, L. *Education and Identity.* (2nd ed.) San Francisco: Jossey-Bass, 1993.

Cortés, C. E. "The Diversity Within: Intermarriage, Identity, and Campus Community." *About Campus,* 2000, *5*, 5–10.

DaCosta, K. M. "Multiracial Identity: From Personal Problem to Public Issue." In L. I. Winters and H. L. DeBose (eds.), *New Faces in a Changing America: Multiracial Identity in the Twenty-First Century.* Thousand Oaks, Calif.: Sage, 2003.

Daniel, G. R. "Black and White Identity in the New Millennium: Unsevering the Ties That Bind." In M.P.P. Root (ed.), *The Multiracial Experience: Racial Borders as the New Frontier.* Thousand Oaks, Calif.: Sage, 1996.

Diaz, M. "Race Doesn't Exist." In P. F. Gaskins (ed.), *What Are You?* New York: Holt, 1999.

El-Khawas, E. "The Many Dimensions of Student Diversity." In S. R. Komives and D. B. Woodard (eds.), *Student Services: A Handbook For the Profession.* (4th ed.) San Francisco: Jossey-Bass, 2003.

Friedlander, L. J., Reid, G. J., Shupak, N., and Cribbie, R. "Social Support, Self-Esteem, and Stress as Predictors of Adjustment to University Among First-Year Undergraduates." *Journal of College Student Development,* 2007, *48*, 259–274.

Gaskins, P. F. *What Are You?* New York: Holt, 1999.

Hall, C.C.I. "2001: A Race Odyssey." In M.P.P. Root (ed.), *The Multiracial Experience: Racial Borders as the New Frontier.* Thousand Oaks, Calif.: Sage, 1996.

Hall, C.C.I. "Mixed-Race Women: One More Mountain to Climb." In A. R. Gillem and C. A. Thompson (eds.), *Biracial Women in Therapy: Between the Rock of Gender and the Hard Place of Race.* New York: Haworth Press, 2004.

India. "I Just Say I'm Native American." In P. F. Gaskins (ed.), *What Are You?* New York: Holt, 1999.

Israel, T. "Conversations, Not Categories: The Intersection of Biracial and Bisexual Identities." *Women and Therapy,* 2004, *27*, 173–184.

Jones, N. A., and Smith, A. S. "The Two or More Races Population: 2000." Washington, D.C.: U.S. Census Bureau, 2001.

Josselson, R. *Revising Herself: The Story of Women's Identity from College to Midlife.* New York: Oxford University Press, 1996.

Kellogg, A. "Exploring Critical Incidents in the Racial Identity of Multiracial College Students." Unpublished doctoral dissertation, University of Iowa, 2006.

Kenney, K. R. "Counseling Interracial Couples and Multiracial Individuals: Applying a Multiracial Counseling Competency Framework." *Counseling and Human Development,* 2002, *35*, 1–13.

King, A. R. "Uncertainty and Evolution: Contributions to Identity Development for Female College Students Who Identify as Multiracial/Biracial–Bisexual/Pansexual." Unpublished doctoral dissertation, Iowa State University, 2008.

Lickel, B., and others. "Varieties of Groups and the Perceptions of Group Entitativity." *Journal of Personality and Social Psychology,* 2000, *78*, 223–246.

Miville, M., Constantine, M., Baysden, M., and So-Lloyd, G. "Chameleon Changes: An Exploration of Racial Identity Themes of Multiracial People." *Journal of Counseling Psychology,* 2005, *52*, 507–516.

Multicultural Student Affairs. "Learning Communities." Iowa State University. Retrieved Mar. 18, 2007, from http://www.dso.iastate.edu/msa/learningcommunities/.

Randolph, D. M. "I'm Black and Korean." In P. F. Gaskins (ed.), *What Are You?* New York: Holt, 1999.

Renn, K. A. "Patterns of Situational Identity Among Biracial and Multiracial College Students." *Review of Higher Education,* 2000, 23, 399–420.

Renn, K. A. "Understanding the Identities of Mixed-Race College Students Through a Developmental Ecology Lens." *Journal of College Student Development,* 2003, 44, 383–403.

Renn, K. A. *Mixed Race Students in College: The Ecology of Race, Identity, and Community on Campus.* Albany, N.Y.: SUNY Press, 2004.

Root, M.P.P. "Resolving the 'Other' Status: Identity Development of Biracial Individuals." *Women and Therapy,* 1990, 9, 185–205.

Sanford, N. *Self and Society: Social Change and Individual Development.* New York: Atherton Press, 1966.

Torres, V. "Knowing Today's and Tomorrow's Students." In G. L. Kramer (ed.), *Fostering Student Success in the Campus Community.* San Francisco: Jossey-Bass, 2007.

Turner, J. C. "Towards a Cognitive Redefinition of the Social Group." In H. Tajfel (ed.), *Social Identity and Intergroup Relations.* Cambridge: Cambridge University Press, 1982.

ALISSA R. KING is a doctoral candidate at Iowa State University and an assistant professor of social sciences at Iowa Central Community College.

5

This chapter summarizes the context for the provision of services and programs for multiracial students and provides three case studies of current practice.

Multiracial Student Services Come of Age: The State of Multiracial Student Services in Higher Education in the United States

Michael Paul A. Wong, Joshua Buckner

After 6.8 million people indicated two or more races on the 2000 U.S. Census (Jones and Smith, 2001), the topics of biraciality and multiraciality have become more visible in the national dialogue about race and identity. As a site where these discussions tend to take on great significance, higher education has been no exception (Jaschik, 2006). The national dialogue on the role and future of biracial and multiracial students has prompted numerous and varied responses from colleges and universities seeking to understand and serve multiracial students better (MultiRacial Network, 2008).

This chapter provides insight into the recent appearance of multiracial student services in U.S. higher education by presenting a review of current practice within student affairs administration. We begin by discussing the historical and social context for multiracial student services within prevailing approaches to multicultural identity development. We follow with three case studies of multiracial student services models. The chapter closes with some implications for student affairs and recommendations for future study.

We are indebted to several individuals who pointed us toward colleges and universities that seemed to be leading in the area of significant and high-quality multiracial student services.

Social and Theoretical Contexts for Multiracial Student Services

The demographic makeup and social climate of the campus play a substantial role in determining the specific needs of the local multiracial population (Kellogg, 2006). Multiracial services are sometimes created in response to a particular issue on campus, such as at the University of Notre Dame, where biracial and transracially adopted students experienced pressure from their peers to choose which culture to celebrate while matriculating. Multiracial people often face societal pressure to claim one primary heritage yet experience exclusion when they attempt to do so (see Chapters Two through Four, this volume). In one study of U.S. college students' attitudes toward multiracial children, White participants believed mixed Black/White children would experience more social acceptance among other Black children, whereas African Americans believed that mixed Black/White children would experience more social acceptance among other White children (Chesley and Wagner, 2003). These social attitudes may leave the multiracial person in a cultural no-man's-land, void of the sense of belonging with a group.

Evidence suggests that in the past generation, attitudes toward multiracial people in the United States have improved (Chesley and Wagner, 2003) as multiracial identity has come to be perceived by many people as a legitimate and distinct identity (Renn, 2004). In some cases, multiracial identity is even viewed as a proficiency, since it allows an advantageous perspective from which to understand the socially constructed aspects of race and ethnicity (Renn, 2004). Theoretical models of multiracial identity development correlate to this shift from deficiency to separate multiracial identity to proficiency (see Chapter Two for more detailed discussion of identity development models).

For the purpose of informing the delivery of multiracial student services, it is important to understand a key distinction among multiracial identity theories, which can be categorized by their descriptions of the highest stage of multiracial identity that can be achieved. According to Renn (2004), most theories end in the achievement of one of three types of identities: an integrated identity, a multiracial identity, or an ability to engage in various "border crossings" (Root, 1996). The common theme among all three sets of theories is the desire to resolve the racial otherness (Root, 1990) created by being born of mixed heritage in a predominantly monoracial society.

The first group of theories (Poston, 1990) holds that a highly developed multiracial person achieves an integrated identity, similar to that found in the final phase of traditional stage-based minority identity models (Cross, 1995; Helms, 1995). At this stage, the multiracial person has achieved a self-awareness that accepts both the positive and negative aspects of being multiracial and views his or her own racial identity as being one component of self. Construction and ownership of a distinctly multiracial identity is the goal of a second group of models (see Root, 1990, 1996). At the end stage of identity development, the healthy individual has identified as a multiracial person rather than identifying with one or more monoracial identities. The third set of multiracial identity models describes a greater ability to engage in "border crossings" (Root, 1996). Depending on the needs of the individual and the racial climate that is present, the multiracial person can (1) passively accept the identity society assigns, (2) claim more than one racial group, (3) claim only one racial group, or (4) claim a unified multiracial identity (Root, 1990). Within this model, the signifier of a healthy identity is the power to consciously choose which method to employ, and even change methods as needed.

The differences among these three groups of theories present a conceptual challenge in implementing multiracial services, since there is no strong consensus on the optimal final phase of multiracial identity. However, although these three groups of identity models differ in their end points, they provide insight into the developmental milestones toward which multiracial college students may be moving. The social landscape and processes of personal identity development that multiracial students navigate provide the backdrop on which multiracial services have been implemented.

Gathering and Organizing Information on Multiracial Student Services

Given the dearth of research on the topic, this chapter is intended as a review of the practice of multiracial student services rather than a review of the literature. We used a snowball approach to data gathering that began with a review of the literature of multiracial student services and progressed through reviews of national and regional Web sites of organizations that specialize in issues of multiracial people. The MAVIN Foundation offered an especially useful database of higher education resources for multiracial people that, although infrequently updated, gave us a starting point to begin exploring individual colleges and universities that seemed to have had strong multiracial programs or student movements at one time. Another important resource was the listserv of the MultiRacial Network (MRN) of the American College Personnel Association's Standing Committee on Multicultural Affairs (MultiRacial Network, 2008). The leadership of the MRN posted our request for information about significant and high-quality multiracial student services at any college or university.

Beginning with this initial, albeit incomplete, list of institutions that either had significant multiracial student services programs at one time or were known to have significant programs, we contacted associated staff or analyzed Web sites for thirty-five institutions that seemed to offer services specifically designed for multiracial students. Some institutions on the initial list had ceased activities in this area, but staff were able to refer us to other institutions with more developed services.

We analyzed this information to construct categories grounded in the data available about these programs. Once we agreed on the categories, we located an institution for each category that could provide access to a student services staff member who might serve as a respondent for interviews. We interviewed three individuals to generate case studies, using a standardized interview protocol and recording the interviews with the permission of the respondent. Some time after the interviews, we contacted the respondents again and shared drafts of the emerging concepts and the resulting manuscript for additional comments and validation. The following sections offer our organizing theories of multiracial student services that emerged from the interviews.

Emerging Practices in Multiracial Student Services

In our analysis of the multiracial student services that we identified at different colleges and universities, the breadth of practice can best be represented as a factor of two components: professional staff assigned by the institution to deliver services to multiracial students and strong student leadership in the community of multiracial students. In the case of professional staff, we found in most cases that these staff were themselves multiracial or had some personal connection to the issue, such as the presence of a close multiracial family member or friend. The stronger programs had formal staff assigned to this issue with clearly articulated responsibilities, such as the multiracial outreach counselors at New York University's Center for Multicultural Education. Some other programs had persisted because of a supportive group of community members from across the campus who volunteered their time to student-run programs as mentors or informal advisers, as in the support group at the University of Notre Dame. The presence of formal staff may have been subtle, as in an existing multicultural support program that incorporated multiracial students as one population that fell under the umbrella of a monoracial target group, without actually assigning staff to address this population. The University of Southern California's Office of Black Student Programs regularly addresses multiracial issues within its programming, without employing a formal position to do this.

The other key factor that seemed to be present in almost every case of multiracial student services that we identified was student leadership. As with the presence of formal staff assigned to multiracial student services, evidence of student leadership varied from a new student organization formed with the explicit goal of raising awareness and support for multiracial students, to self-identified multiracial students taking positions of leadership in existing student organizations or student government (see Chapter Six, this volume). The stronger programs that we identified had regularly occurring programming or services that were dependent on continued participation from student leadership to remain in existence, such as the Mixed Awareness Month and Mixed Awareness Week at George Washington University. The case studies of three programs that follow illustrate the variety of service delivery models that can be found in this matrix.

NEW DIRECTIONS FOR INSTITUTIONAL RESEARCH • DOI: 10.1002/ss

Case Studies of Multiracial Student Services

The University of Colorado (CU) at Boulder's Center for Multicultural Affairs is an example of a service model that pairs formal staff assigned to multiracial student programming with the involvement of student leadership. Our respondent recalled the center's origins as an Educational Opportunity Program office that, after many restructuring processes, eventually reorganized into its current form as a generalized multicultural support program. She pointed out that the center rewrote its mission statement to include multiracial students and assigned formal staff to provide services to that student identity group. The respondent described the reestablishment of the multiracial student organization as concurrent with this reorganization. The student organization was described as having changed from an insular group of students interested primarily in mutual support to a student organization whose members were involved in high-profile leadership positions in other multicultural student organizations and campuswide student government.

The respondent described the current form of CU Boulder's Center for Multicultural Affairs as delivering a set of programs equally to each served racial group and including peer education, retention support services, programming that included a month-long celebration of the group, and advising to the group's student leaders. She emphasized that multiracial students were targeted for services on an equal footing with American Indian, African American, Asian Pacific American, and Chicano/Latino students. As she described it, as with the other groups, a university counselor was assigned, albeit shared with Asian Pacific American students, to provide services to multiracial students.

In our analysis, which was supported in subsequent follow-up questions with the respondent, the presence of both formal staff support and a working student organization generated a symbiotic relationship. The multiracial counselor provided support to student leadership to ensure that the organization persisted and individual students were mentored to increase their leadership skills. And the student organization provided support to the larger multicultural community and the Center for Multicultural Affairs by helping to raise awareness about multiracial issues among other student organizations that fall under the center and participate in the annual multiracial event.

The respondent recalled that before the reorganization of the Center for Multicultural Affairs and assignment of staff to multiracial student services, previous versions of the multiracial student organization were founded but did not persist. She remembered that the organizations had isolated themselves from potential alliances and opportunities to raise campus awareness among their fellow student organizations. Eventually the earlier incarnations of the multiracial student organization collapsed from within when the membership split around issues of identity and purpose. To the respondent, the presence of a set of formal programs with dedicated staff time assigned created a stabilizing influence and attention to student leaders'

NEW DIRECTIONS FOR INSTITUTIONAL RESEARCH • DOI: 10.1002/ss

learning and identity development; conversely, the set of services was organized so that they could not be successfully administered without an active group of student leaders from the multiracial student community.

A respondent at Brown University's Third World Center (TWC) described another model in which paid student programmers coordinated multiracial programming under the supervision of professional staff. In the respondent's description, the TWC provided support to students by sponsoring cultural heritage weeks and months and offering programs that target all students of color, such as a Third World Transition Program and residential Minority Peer Counselor Program. Within this model, according to the respondent, multiracial student services were delivered alongside services for other students of color to promote ethnic pluralism, increase cultural awareness, facilitate community building, and provide assistance with college transition.

The respondent described Brown University's Multiracial Heritage Week, which, like other heritage weeks and months, was sponsored by the TWC and led by two student programmers who worked under the guidance and supervision of TWC professional staff. According to the respondent, Multiracial Heritage Week began in 1993 and included a diverse series of panel discussions, lectures, performances, and other activities designed to address multiracial issues, support multiracial students in their development, and strengthen relations with other ethnic communities. He recalled past Multiracial Heritage Weeks that included events such as a panel discussion on transracial adoption, an artistic exhibition fusing multiple cultural traditions, and a keynote address by a multiracial advocate. In his description, the multiracial student programmers partnered with interested student organizations on campus, most notably the Brown University Organization of Multiracial and Biracial Students and the Brown University Hapa Club. According to the respondent, heritage week events also benefited from active collaboration with multiracial faculty and cocurricular departments who participate in or sponsor the activities. He described funding for these events as coming from multiple sources: various ethnic program offices sponsor events, and the student board responsible for allocating funds from the student activities fee distributed a portion of student fees to the heritage weeks. In our analysis of national practices, in recognizing multiracial students as a distinct ethnic group, Brown University offered a high level of support to multiracial students compared to the support offered at other colleges that we identified.

The respondent described other programs intended to show consciousness of the needs of multiracial students. He described the Third World Transition Program, an orientation program aimed at students of color, as providing students with an environment that encouraged self-identification, including opportunities for multiracial students to claim a positive multiracial identity. To the respondent, multiracial participants in this program were encouraged to validate their multiracial identity, as well as any other identities that students believed best describe them. The Minority Peer Counselor Program helped incoming students of color seek support through peer mentoring and exposure to campus resources. The respondent emphasized that a culturally diverse student staff played a large role in both of these programs. To the respondent, the inclusion of multiracial student staff in these programs enhanced assistance to multiracial students and awareness of multiracial issues. He asserted that at Brown University, services for students of color explicitly included multiracial student services in name and deed.

The respondent described Brown University's TWC as listing multiracial students specifically in its mission statement and treating them as a distinct community served by the department while also allowing these students to claim other ethnic identities if they wish. Moreover, he maintained that support provided to multiracial students was nearly equal to the support offered to other targeted ethnicities. Student affairs professional staff did not deliver multiracial services directly. Instead, according to the respondent, paid student programmers produced these services within the context of the TWC mission and structure.

According to a third respondent, like many other multicultural student services offices and specific ethnic group support offices, Chicano Latino Student Programs at Loyola Marymount University in Los Angeles had interest in multiracial student issues among the staff but little student leadership participation in the issue. Nevertheless, she continued, the staff made a visible commitment to supporting multiracial students by acknowledging multiracial Chicano and Latino students in the departmental mission statement and providing services to this community. She asserted that along with national origin, religion, gender, class, linguistic orientation, and sexual orientation, biraciality and ethnic identity were explicitly valued as essential aspects of this cultural group's inherent diversity.

As at CU Boulder and Brown University, multiracial student services at Loyola Marymount Chicano Latino Student Programs developed within its local context. In the respondent's description of this context, although the multiracial student community was neither advocating for itself nor formally organized within the Chicano Latino student community, local student affairs staff and their allies had enough personal and professional interest in exploring issues of student multiraciality to offer programming around this issue. Although she noted the absence of a more formal staff commitment to provide programming, she described services that were delivered through individual activities or events, albeit with little to no connection to a larger programming or educational philosophy, sometimes with participation from an individual community member. Optimistically, as we compared the development of this institution's practices to that of others that we have identified, the programming that does take place might, as in the case of other institutions that we studied, deliver student reflection and genuine learning, such that future generations of student leaders who identify as Chicano Latino and multiracial might be in a better position to build partnerships with these supportive staff to create larger scale formal programming.

NEW DIRECTIONS FOR INSTITUTIONAL RESEARCH • DOI: 10.1002/ss

Chicano Latino Student Programs at Loyola Marymount is not unlike many other multiracial student services providers that we identified that generate programming with neither the formal participation of student leadership nor formal staff assigned to support multiracial students. The service delivery model of single events without long-term institutional commitment, such as a student-sponsored conference at Michigan State University, the biracial support group at Pennsylvania State University, or the inclusion of multiracial students in a multicultural center's mission statement without assigned staff was the most common model of multiracial student services that we identified. We consider these efforts to be the beginning stages of a local movement, shaped by local campus culture and history, that will eventually result in discussion of multiracial students in the context of campuswide support for all students' multicultural identity development.

Conclusion

The presence of formally assigned professional staff can provide multiracial services with increased depth, continuity, and historical perspective, as described by our respondent at CU Boulder. As described by our respondent at Brown University, the presence of an established multiracial student organization and strong student leadership can provide a forum for students to advocate, engage in dialogue with the institution, and serve one another. At Loyola Marymount University, our respondent pointed out the possibility that the delivery of multiracial student services within the context of services targeted toward a single ethnic group can generate needed dialogue about the fluidity of racial and ethnic identity, as well as encourage multiracial students to explore their own identity. Other notable services aside from the three case studies that we identified include multiracial student outreach (New York University), multiracial discussion groups (Notre Dame, Penn State), mixed-race awareness months or weeks (George Washington University), and multiracial adoptee panels (Anderson University). The field of multiracial student services that we were able to locate is marked by variation in both philosophy and practice.

Existing multiracial identity development models provide a few initial views of the path of multiracial student development. Our respondents agreed that the demographics and histories of the local population vary; consequently, the needs of the multiracial student population vary. According to all three respondents, there is also a large degree of diversity within the multiracial community itself. These variables require student affairs professionals to exercise flexibility in their vision of multiracial services and remain open to advances in both theory and practice.

Most of the programs that we identified were recently founded, and few practitioners we interviewed were aware of similar efforts taking place at other institutions. The multiracial student services that we found have set precedents in supporting multiracial students in their college experiences. However, based on the limited number of existing programs and the newness of the underlying theoretical constructs, it is difficult to determine a set of best practices for multiracial services at this time. We hope that this overview of existing services and their success will encourage others to generate their own models of multiracial student services on more college campuses.

References

Chesley, G. L., and Wagner, W. G. "Adults' Attitudes Toward Multiracial Children." *Journal of Black Psychology,* 2003, *29,* 463–480.

Cross, W. E., Jr. "The Psychology of Nigrescence: Revisiting the Cross Model." In J. G. Ponterotto, J. M. Casas, L. A. Suzuki, and C. M. Alexander (eds.), *Handbook of Multicultural Counseling.* Thousand Oaks, Calif.: Sage, 1995.

Helms, J. E. "An Update of Helms's White and People of Color Racial Identity Development Models." In J. G. Ponterotto, J. M. Casas, L. A. Suzuki, and C. M. Alexander (eds.), *Handbook of Multicultural Counseling.* Thousand Oaks, Calif.: Sage, 1995.

Jaschik, S. "An End to Picking One Box." *Inside Higher Ed,* Aug. 8, 2006. Retrieved Mar. 22, 2008, from http://www.insidehighered.com/news/2006/08/08/race.

Jones, N. A., and Smith, A. S. "The Two or More Races Population: 2000." Washington D.C.: U.S. Census Bureau, 2001.

Kellogg, A. "Exploring Critical Incidents in the Racial Identity of Multiracial College Students." Unpublished doctoral dissertation, University of Iowa, 2006.

MultiRacial Network. "MultiRacial Network (MRN)." Retrieved Mar. 22, 2008, from http://www.myacpa.org/sc/scma/mrn_home.cfm.

Poston, W.S.C. "The Biracial Identity Development Model: A Needed Addition." *Journal of Counseling and Development,* 1990, *69,* 152–155.

Renn, K. A. *Mixed Race Students in College: The Ecology of Race, Identity, and Community on Campus.* Albany, N.Y.: SUNY Press, 2004.

Root, M.P.P. "Resolving 'Other' Status: Identity Development of Biracial Individuals." *Women and Therapy,* 1990, *9*(1/2), 185–205.

Root, M.P.P. *The Multiracial Experience: Racial Borders as the New Frontier.* Thousand Oaks, Calif.: Sage, 1996.

MICHAEL PAUL A. WONG *is director of the Learning Center at the University of California, Riverside.*

JOSHUA BUCKNER *coordinates the Assistance, Counseling, and Encouragement and Summer Bridge Programs at the University of California, Riverside.*

NEW DIRECTIONS FOR INSTITUTIONAL RESEARCH • DOI: 10.1002/ss

6

This chapter reviews relevant literature on multiracial student organizations, highlights challenges faced by such groups, and provides suggestions for advisers who work with members and leaders of multiracial campus groups.

The Space in Between: Issues for Multiracial Student Organizations and Advising

C. Casey Ozaki, Marc Johnston

Originating with the civil rights movement, campus organizations for students of color were established on predominantly White campuses to help them meet other students from similar racial and ethnic backgrounds, have a safe space to identify with and share issues related to their race and ethnicity, and provide a group to advocate for their needs (Young and Hannon, 2002). Over time, such organizations have established themselves as permanent aspects of extracurricular campus life, but as the number of mixed-race students has grown on campuses, a new type of student organization has developed to respond to multiracial students' needs (Taniguchi and Heidenreich, 2005).

While multiracial organizations occur on campuses in increasing numbers, little is known about how they develop and function and the purposes they serve for students. Yet as these organizations become more prevalent, staff, administrators, and faculty are being asked to work with and advise them. In this chapter, we briefly review what is known about multiracial and identity-based student organizations, discuss some of the issues and challenges unique to them, and provide suggestions for working with and advising them.

Throughout this chapter, we use the terms *mixed race* and *multiracial* interchangeably. We also use the term *hapa* frequently with regard to multiracial individuals and groups, originating in Hawaii in reference

NEW DIRECTIONS FOR STUDENT SERVICES, no. 123, Fall 2008 © Wiley Periodicals, Inc.
Published online in Wiley InterScience (www.interscience.wiley.com) • DOI: 10.1002/ss.286

to individuals of Hawaiian and Caucasian heritage. Currently, *hapa* is often used to refer to anyone of a racially mixed Asian heritage, and even more recently to anyone who is of mixed-race heritage (Taniguchi and Heidenreich, 2005). Within this chapter, *hapa* refers to mixed Asian heritage.

Background

Although student involvement and leadership have been well studied, knowledge of the development and functioning of multiracial student organizations continues to emerge. This increasing population of students requires that faculty, staff, and administrators be conversant with the issues that mixed-race students experience and understand how to work with such organizations within the campus structure. This section briefly discusses research about the development and functioning of multiracial student organizations and identity-based organizations in general.

Development. Students enter and become involved with multiracial and identity-based student organizations for a multitude of reasons. Social, political, and psychological explanations are all cited in the literature as factors that prompt student involvement in these organizations and are more salient as students take on various roles. First, students identify socializing as a major reason for wanting to participate in identity-based organizations (Renn, 2007; Renn and Ozaki, 2005). In a study exploring the development of a hapa multiracial student organization, Ozaki (2004) found that students overwhelmingly sought to meet new people and be involved with social activities in conjunction with wanting to be in a setting where a majority of people were hapa. Second, many students cite the desire to have more of a political voice as an impetus for involvement. Many leaders who began identity-based groups, including leaders of multiracial student groups, talk about not feeling welcome in other groups on campus or wanting a venue to advocate for issues related to their group (Harper and Quaye, 2007; Ozaki, 2004; Renn and Ozaki, 2005). Finally, in studies of identity-based student groups, members and leaders state that they are looking for a space to express and explore their identity in relationship to the particular characteristic of the group (Renn, 2007; Renn and Ozaki, 2005). Specifically, members of multiracial organizations cite wanting a space on campus where mixed-race students can share their similar experiences and backgrounds (Ozaki, 2004).

Leadership. Leaders of multiracial and identity-based groups have a particularly important role in the development and operation of these organizations. Renn (2000) suggested that three factors must be present for a multiracial student organization to develop on a campus: (1) there must be a critical mass of students interested in and seeing the need for such a group, (2) students n ed to identify the need for a space to express and explore their multiracial identity, and (3) they must feel that they do not belong to the monoracial groups on campus. It is the latter two factors that are often recognized and championed by future group leaders (Ozaki, 2004; Renn and Ozaki, 2005). At times this was because they felt the monoracial group was unwelcoming, but often it was that they felt that the monoracial and mono- cultural groups did not reflect their biracial and bicultural backgrounds, and therefore they did not see themselves in existing groups on campus (Ozaki, 2004).

Existing studies also emphasize the reciprocal relationship between leadership and identity development of group members (Renn, 2007; Renn and Ozaki, 2005). In a study of lesbian, gay, bisexual, and transgender stu- dent organizations and leaders, Renn (2007) found that a cyclical pattern developed as students became more involved and invested in the organiza- tions. The involvement-identification cycle describes a pattern of students' increased involvement, which leads to increased public and personal iden- tification and results in increased leadership.

Furthermore, the organization's leadership can have a significant impact on the mission, character, and even membership of the group (Ozaki, 2004; Renn and Ozaki, 2005). The leaders who become involved contribute to the activities the organizations engage in and shape the goals of the orga- nization. For example, a group whose leader sees the organization as a venue to advocate for the needs of multiracial students is more likely to be political in nature versus the group whose leader wants to cultivate a space to help students explore their identity. The activities in which the group is involved affect the type of students it attracts.

Role of Adviser. Although few studies focus on the role of advisers in multiracial or identity-based groups, some studies have indicated that the level of involvement of an adviser can have a positive impact on individu- als and groups. Research on identity-based student organizations found that advisers can function as a facilitator for the development of individual mem- bers and the group itself. Leaders of groups that received support, informa- tion, and resources from an an adviser felt encouraged to continue their efforts (Renn, 2007; Renn and Ozaki, 2005). Furthermore, students state that through encouragement and interaction with faculty advisers, they chose to become involved with the organization and eventually pursue lead- ership within the group (Renn, 2007).

Common Challenges and Issues for Multiracial Student Organizations

Multiracial student organizations may face unique and different challenges. In addition, although they may experience issues similar to those faced by monoracial groups and groups not based on identity, multiracial student organizations may experience them more often.

Leader and Member Identity Conflict. First, mixed-race students may find themselves facing some unique issues, many of which deal with the diversity of personal and group identities within the *mixed race* umbrella term. Root (1996) claimed that the naming of one's identity is an important step in self-empowerment and validation of one's existence as a multiracial individual. Whether it be *mixed, multiracial, biracial, Black and Asian, human,* or in Tiger Woods's case, *Cablinasian* (a term he made up to describe his heritage: Caucasian, Black, American-Indian, and Asian), these terms have salience to students and can often help to recruit or deter others from being involved in the organization. For example, one student organization could be called the Multiracial Student Association, while another organization is named Biracial Students Circle. The term *biracial* often can exclude students who may claim heritages in more than two racial groups. In addition, *multiracial* may exclude students who identify as multiethnic or mixed in other ways. These nuances are often what students in these organizations deal with when creating and maintaining such groups.

Second, conflicts may develop within multiracial student organizations when the identities of the group leaders differ from those of the general members. If the leader of the group has a certain identity and perspective on multiraciality, that person can run the risk of alienating others who do not share the same common set of beliefs about race but may be of mixed race. This reflects a common notion that the goals of identity-based groups largely depend on the identity of their leaders (Renn and Ozaki, 2005). Some leaders may be more politically conscious, and the respective groups they lead may also reflect their level of awareness. These differences may lead to challenges in meeting the needs of students who seek involvement in the group for a support system versus students who want the group to be more politically active. The tool kit provided by Campus Awareness + Compliance Initiative (CACI; Padilla, 2004) recommends that new organizations try to provide a group that will meet the needs of students who are looking for a space to explore their multiracial identity as well as those who want to be more politically active and advocate for multiracial student needs. Organizations that provide a "safe space" in addition to being active politically will most likely reap increased membership and sustainability because they will be meeting the needs of the greatest number of students.

Third, challenges may arise when the leaders of multiracial groups do not share the same mixed heritage as other members within the group. For example, a diverse group of multiracial individuals may come together to start a new organization they call the Multiracial Student Alliance. The leaders of the group filter their experiences and needs through their hapa identity, while the majority of the general membership classify themselves as biracial (Black/White) and consider their needs and experiences through this particular racial mix. Whether it is personality differences or racial politics, this situation can create division within the larger group. This was the case when the Hapa Asian Pacific Alliance was created at Michigan State University in 2001. The founders felt that students of mixed Asian heritage had their own unique set of needs and thus established a group focused on the hapa experience independent from a broader multiracial student group.

Hapa-based student organizations and broader-based multiracial organizations are found throughout the nation. These organizations want to create a community or pan-ethnicity for individuals of mixed Asian heritage; however, they also prevent broader multiracial organizing and have been referred to as exclusive and elitist (Taniguchi and Heidenreich, 2005).

Conflicts with Monoracial Student of Color Groups. Not only can differences between hapa and broader multiracial organizations create challenges for campuses, but issues may arise between multiracial organizations and traditional monoracial student-of-color groups. Many institutions provide services and organizations that traditionally target four racial minority groups: African American/Black, Chicano/Latino/Hispanic, Native American/American Indian, and Asian American/Pacific Islander. Current monoracial student-of-color groups, like Asian American associations, can create communities that may not be perceived as inclusive of multiracial students. Mixed-race students who create their own multiracial organizations often cite feelings of not being "[insert racial term here] enough" for the monoracial groups (Renn, 2000, 2004).

There can be a sense of competition for resources when multiracial groups form on campuses with long histories of monoracial student of color organizations. On predominantly White campuses, resources may already feel limited for students of color, who may sense they have to share another piece of the pie with yet another group of students. Notions of authenticity can create hostile environments between various groups, and identity politics can lead to disenfranchisement or divisiveness on campuses, especially when the multiracial movement has been charged with the potential of diluting numbers of traditional minority groups and undermining programs such as affirmative action (Williams, 2003).

High Turnover Rate. The MAVIN Foundation's CACI created an online tool kit for mixed-race student groups in which a major focus was that of the transition from one leadership group to another. The tool kit addresses the all-too-common scenario of a group of dedicated students coming together to form a new student organization that has a few years of success but then dies out because of a lack of cultivating future leadership for the group (Padilla, 2004). Although this issue is not solely a problem facing multiracial student organizations, it may seem amplified given the high turnover rates of these on-campus groups.

Since groups largely reflect the identity of their leaders, the groups may take on different goals and objectives once the leaders graduate. Often there is a lack of strategic planning during initial creation of the group, including establishing vision and goals. While many organizations cite the goal of building community, there are no strategic plans on how to obtain this goal (Renn, 2007).

NEW DIRECTIONS FOR STUDENT SERVICES • DOI: 10.1002/ss

How Student Affairs Professionals Can Support Multiracial Students and Their Organizations

Whether as an official adviser for a multiracial student organization, someone working in multicultural affairs, or possibly someone just interested in multiracial students and their organizations, there are several areas where student affairs professionals can support multiracial students' organizations. Following are ten suggestions for working with multiracial students and their organizations:

1. *Assist students in focusing on the vision and goals for the organization.* As recommended by CACI's tool kit (Padilla, 2004), focusing on clarifying the vision and goals of the organization may help with increasing membership and decreasing turnover rates. As an adviser, you can assist students to identify the best methods for creating a vision and strategic plan toward that vision, as well as hold the students accountable as they progress toward their goals. This may be as simple as asking how a proposed program, like the so-called date auctions that are popular on some campuses, aligns with their possible goal of building community.

2. *Advocate for multiracial issues and not just the student organization.* Although advocacy is an extremely important tool in supporting multiracial students on campus, longer-lasting benefits may be found when advocating for multiracial issues, not just students. For example, by supporting the right of students to check more than one racial/ethnic identity box on campus surveys or challenging ethnic-based support programs that do not explicitly include multiracial students, you can help create a more inclusive campus environment for multiracial students. Advocating for broader multiracial issues also has the potential to plant seeds in colleagues' heads about potential changes they can make that will have a broader impact. Advocating just for the student organization may leave out potential benefits that could also reach students who are not involved in the organization.

3. *Help students navigate potential racial politics on campus.* Advisers can assist new student organizations with the necessary steps to create a new organization on campus: writing a constitution and filing it with the student activities office, for example. In addition, advisers may need to assist students by teaching them the necessary tools to advocate for themselves and navigate conflicts that may arise due to racial politics on campus. Student groups are often focused on building community through social gatherings and discussions of shared experiences related to being multiracial. However, there may be a lack of discussion of specific issues of racism and racial oppression. By helping students to examine race and openly discuss issues related to racism, professionals may help multiracial students gain a better understanding of why others may be hesitant to support their group's formation and future success.

NEW DIRECTIONS FOR STUDENT SERVICES • DOI: 10.1002/ss

4. *Assess your own racial identity and personal biases about multiracial identity.* By reflecting on your own racial identity and how you came to identify that way, you may be better prepared to assist students in their own personal journeys of identity development and why they may be so passionate about their safe space on campus. You can assess your own thoughts and biases around multiracial identity as well by asking yourself questions such as, "Do I believe there should be a separate multiracial category on the U.S. Census?" and "Do I feel that multiracial individuals need more help than others?"

5. *Understand how your identity may be perceived by students.* Students may perceive your personal racial identity and beliefs about multiracial identity as possible areas of solidarity or conflict. Advisers must be aware that their identity may have an impact on their effectiveness as an adviser. Students may question whether your views on multiraciality are their own, and conflicts may arise due to those differences, whether real or perceived. By understanding the impact of your identity on the relationships you build with students, you will be one step ahead in confronting conflicts that may arise.

6. *Create opportunities for dialogue between leaders of multiracial and monoracial student organizations.* Advisers of multiracial student organizations may also find it helpful to create opportunities for dialogue about multiracial students and identity in which leaders of all groups are invited and potential areas of conflict can be brought into the open in a facilitated manner. Reaching out to the advisers of monoracial groups to discuss issues at hand will help all parties involved understand the need for dialogue and collaboration.

7. *Help students to understand the differences among race, ethnicity, and culture.* Advisers may be able to help students better understand the nuances among the terms *race, ethnicity,* and *culture* and why it is important to have a clear understanding of these topics and how they relate to identity.

8. *Be aware of resources on the mixed-race experience so you can better inform students.* Advisers who are familiar with resources on the mixed-race experience will be able to provide better support for students who may need extra support while they are exploring their multiracial identity. Such resources include national advocacy groups like the MAVIN Foundation, Association of Multi-Ethnic Americans, and Swirl, Inc., and books such as *Mixed Race Students in College* (Renn, 2004) and *The Multiracial Experience* (Root, 1996).

9. *Keep in mind the potential and important impact you can have on the development and sustainability of organizations and their individual members.* At times the adviser's role can appear to be reduced to a mandatory signature for the organization, but advisers can have an impact on individual students and the group itself through their position. Advisers can keep in mind the importance of their role as educator, facilitator,

counselor, and resource for students and organizations that are continually developing and changing.

10. *Be open to change.* Just as the overall student population continues to change in terms of demographics and ways of thinking, so will the multiracial student population. We are seeing more students who identify as multigeneration multiracial or who come from long lineages of interracial or interethnic mixing. New ideologies about race and culture may continue to grow, like the opting out of racial categorization altogether (Renn, 2004). Student affairs professionals working with multiracial students should not only be open to change but should expect it.

Conclusion

This chapter aims to educate faculty, administrators, and staff on the unique dynamics involved in the development and functioning of multiracial student organizations. The information about existing research on multiracial and identity-based student organizations provides a base for being fully informed about their development and functioning. The challenges facing multiracial student organizations are both issues confronted by many student organizations in general and issues unique to the multiracial population on campus. As these organizations become more prevalent and the multiracial student population increases, faculty and staff must be aware of the unique challenges they face as individuals and in formalized university organizations. Advisers are in the position to have a significant impact on the individuals who participate in these groups and the groups themselves. Through thoughtful education and sensitive encouragement and interaction, advisers have the potential to help create an environment on campus for multiracial students to explore their identities, develop socially, and cultivate their voices.

References

Harper, S. R., and Quaye, S. J. "Student Organizations as Venues for Black Identity Expression and Development Among African American Male Student Leaders." *Journal of College Student Development,* 2007, 48, 127–144.

Ozaki, C. K. "The Hapa Student Community: The Creation of a Multiracial Student Organization and Its Impact on Identity." Master's thesis, University of Southern California, 2004.

Padilla, A. "Campus Advocacy and Compliance Initiative: Student Toolkit, 2004." Retrieved Aug. 19, 2007, from http://www.mixituponcampus.org/.

Renn, K. A. "Patterns of Situational Identity Among Biracial and Multiracial College Students." *Review of Higher Education,* 2000, 23, 399–420.

Renn, K. A. *Mixed Race Students in College: The Ecology of Race, Identity, and Community on Campus.* Albany, N.Y.: SUNY Press, 2004.

Renn, K. A. "LGBT Student Leaders and Queer Activists: Identities of Lesbian, Gay, Bisexual, Transgender and Queer Identified College Student Leaders and Activists." *Journal of College Student Development,* 2007, 48, 311–330.

Renn, K. A., and Ozaki, C. K. "Student Leaders in Identity-Based Campus Contexts." Paper presented at the annual meeting of the Association for the Study of Higher Education, Philadelphia, Nov. 2005.

Root, M.P.P. "A Bill of Rights for Racially Mixed People." In M.P.P. Root (ed.), *The Multiracial Experience: Racial Borders as the New Frontier.* Thousand Oaks, Calif.: Sage, 1996.

Taniguchi, A. S., and Heidenreich, L. "Re-Mix: Rethinking the Use of 'Hapa' in Mixed-race Asian/Pacific Islander American Community Organizing." *WSU McNair Journal, Fall* 2005, 135–146.

Williams, K. M. "From Civil Right to the Multiracial Movement." In L. I. Winters and H. L. DeBose (eds.), *New Faces in a Changing America: Multiracial Identity in the Twenty-First Century.* Thousand Oaks, Calif.: Sage, 2003.

Young, L. W., and Hannon, M. D. "The Staying Power of Black Cultural Centers." *Black Issues in Higher Education,* 2002, *18* (2002). Retrieved June 21, 2008, from http://findarticles.com/p/articles/mi_m0DXK/is_26_18/ai_83663853?tag=artBody;col1.

C. CASEY OZAKI is a doctoral candidate at Michigan State University in the Higher, Adult, and Lifelong Education program.

MARC JOHNSTON is director of Asian Pacific American Student Affairs at the University of Arizona.

This chapter presents an overview of current technology trends and how multiracial students' use of these tools may differ from that of their monoracial peers. Implications for student affairs practice and limitations of technology are presented.

7

Being Multiracial in a Wired Society: Using the Internet to Define Identity and Community on Campus

Heather Shea Gasser

Can online communities contribute to a student's sense of belonging? Does the use of new Internet technologies enhance an individual's sense of self? Is one's racial identity relevant in cyberspace? For multiracial students, the answer to these questions is increasingly yes. Whether mixed-race students are more tech savvy than their monoracial peers may be difficult to assert with certainty. However, the proliferation of multiracial groups on social networking sites shows that students look to online portals for a shared experience and supportive community. It is increasingly hard to deny the importance the Internet plays in the identity and social development of students on campus.

This chapter provides a starting point for student affairs practitioners seeking to understand the Internet's role in identity and community development among multiracial individuals on campus. I begin with an overview of current online tools that college students use, address how students' use of these technologies may be contributing to their unique sense of self and community, and conclude with implications for practitioners seeking to use technology for outreach.

Technology Trends

Since the inception of its widespread use on college campuses in the mid-1990s, the Internet has had a tremendous impact on the lives of college

NEW DIRECTIONS FOR STUDENT SERVICES, no. 123, Fall 2008   © Wiley Periodicals, Inc.
Published online in Wiley InterScience (www.interscience.wiley.com) • DOI: 10.1002/ss.287

students (Young, 2001; Kvavik & Caruso, 2005). Their use of technology not only assists them on campus, but may also partially define the college experience of this generation. The Internet is a place where students investigate future careers, find sources for research papers, submit work to be checked for plagiarism, interact with professors outside class using course management portals, or take entire classes exclusively online (Kvavik & Caruso, 2005; Lloyd, Dean, and Cooper, 2007). In their free time, many students use the Internet to express themselves creatively, share their beliefs, engage in dialogue with others, and define (and redefine) themselves (Jones, 2002). Just a decade ago, these developmental processes might have occurred locally on campus in real time (in the residence hall lounge or the student union, or during a student club meeting) and could be witnessed or occasionally affected by student affairs practitioners. Increasingly these forms of student expression and development are hidden from direct observation unless student affairs practitioners are familiar with the tools themselves and can engage students in conversation about what happens online (Wilson, 2007).

As this volume is being published, new uses of the Internet and digital devices are already reaching and being eagerly consumed by the tech-savvy students. Concurrently, the technology in vogue today is either undergoing the process of adoption by the masses, slowly plateauing, or perhaps fading from general use, only to be replaced by new media. Therefore, to give a detailed description of the most frequently used tools makes little sense for the long-term usefulness of this chapter. Nevertheless, a few Internet trends seem to have staying power and are worth describing in more detail.

Social Networking Sites. In general, FaceBook, MySpace, and similar other sites allow registered users to create online profiles for themselves with a personal Web page. Users can write a basic "about me" description, upload photos, create blog entries, rank music and movie preferences, and portray a self-image they want others to see on this individual site. The social networking aspect of the sites occurs when users add friends and join groups. Individual users can leave public or private messages on other users' pages, engage in live chat, and participate in various groups and events.

Generally these sites do not charge a fee for membership because revenue is generated from the advertising banners. Sites like FaceBook and MySpace garner attention from campus administrators because students' behavior and online postings may be subject to observation unless privacy controls are employed (Wilson, 2007). To gauge the scope of FaceBook alone, the site's online fact sheet notes over 69 million active members (http://www.facebook.com/press/info.php?factsheet (Facebook Factsheet, 2008) "in over 40,000 geographic, work-related, collegiate, and high school networks, and . . . ranks as the seventh-most trafficked site in the United States" ("Microsoft and FaceBook," 2006). Whether social networking sites' popularity has reached a plateau on college campuses is still up for debate.

For multiracial students, online social networking sites may offer opportunities for connection and community building when local student organizations or supportive communities do not exist on their campus. When I conducted a search on FaceBook for groups with *multiracial* in the title, I discovered over 163 global groups, some of them with hundreds of members from all over the world.

Wikis. At first glance, a wiki seems like any other informative Web site: a portal for resources and information, a search function, and endless links (Jaschik, 2007). What makes a wiki different is that it employs a unique type of software that allows any user to edit the content (specifically text) on the site. Therefore, the resulting information is collaboratively created by the readers themselves. Errors may be changed to reflect accuracy, and what ideally emerges is the most current and most accurate resource. The best-known wiki is Wikipedia, which proclaims itself to be "an encyclopedia that anyone can edit."

The relevance of the wiki for the multiracial population is the emergent shared experience and solidarity created by the process of developing collaborative content. A recent search of the term *multiracial* in Wikipedia provided a variety of external links, references, and detailed background information. Each entry also contains a discussion page, and on this topic, several individuals disputed the reputability of the content of the article and even suggested its deletion from Wikipedia altogether. It is this opportunity for online dialogue and collaboration that lends merit to the wiki concept.

Other uses of the online collaborative concept known as the wiki include sites developed by student groups on campuses, company intranets, classroom discussion or project sites, and depositories for various information (everything from scholarly publications, statistics, and data to memoirs). The long-term usefulness of a wiki is only as good as the administrators and community of users and contributors. And many dispute the wiki's usefulness as a citable source because the information is not attributable to any one author. Jaschick (2007) noted that "professors have complained about the lack of accuracy or completeness of entries, and some have discouraged or tried to bar students from using it" because "material on Wikipedia—while convenient—may not be trustworthy" (para. 2).

The Blog. A blog (short for Web log) is a Web site where users can post commentary, news, and photos and video. Many are used as online diaries or journals. Some are interactive and allow readers to enter their own comments on the content. Blogs have become popular political and social tools, and many sites, particularly news media, employ them as an opportunity for running commentary about the content of the site.

For multiracial students, the use of the blog is an opportunity for self-expression, feedback, and validation. Blogs are commonly found connected to social networking sites, and students may write and receive feedback from their immediate peer group. Other blogs are stand-alone Web sites that can be easily found by putting the word *blog* after any subject in a search engine. Blogs may also be used for the purpose of student activism. The Web site CampusActivism.org has a number of links to activist blogs (www.campusactivism.org/blog/), and the online magazine www.wiretap-mag.org has contained several articles about mixed-race concerns.

Other Technology Trends. The newest technology can become obsolete within months, and the speed with which new technologies emerge is accelerating. Nevertheless, other trends are worth mentioning for their relevance for the multiracial student population. Sites that allow users to share video (YouTube is the most notable) are, like social networking sites, an opportunity for self-expression. These sites are becoming more and more user friendly, and video clips that are current, practical, or outrageous garner significant attention from a worldwide audience. A search of YouTube for the terms *multiracial* and *mixed race* identified a number of individual portraits, monologues, and political activism videos. Some appeared to have a particular agenda, like the Mixed-Race Project, while others, like the video "Multiracial Issues," were simply personal stories of the experiences of multiracial individuals.

Another notable tool is the podcast. Podcasts are unique because users are able to subscribe to a particular podcast feed that, when connected to the Internet, signals a computer to automatically download the newest edition and then, with an MP3 player, users can take these video or audio files with them to listen to or view at their leisure. "Mixed Chicks Chat" describes itself as a "weekly talkcast about being racially and culturally mixed."

Biracial and Multiracial Students' Use of Technology

There is no evidence to support an assertion that multiracial individuals use the technology described here at a higher rate than their monoracial peers; however, there is reason to believe that new technologies may provide opportunities for multiracial students to explore their identities.

Achieving balance between challenge and support provides stimulus and capacity for development (Sanford, 1966). For multiracial students, college is often the first time they are "noticeably challenged to define their identity outside the familiar environment of home" (Matsumoto, 1995, p. 6). Furthermore, a multiracial student may be caught in what Root (1992) described as the "squeeze effect." As new people entering new social contexts, "multiracial people experience a 'squeeze' of oppression as people of color and by people of color" (p. 5). For the student to be accepted by either White students or students of color, the person may have to choose one of her or his racial heritages and deny the other. The attempt to assert a truly multiracial identity, in which each of a person's races/ethnicities/cultures is equally valuable, may raise questions of loyalty from monoracial groups (Root, 1992). These situations represent challenges to identity.

Technology and the proliferation of online communities may provide support and make the squeeze effect less noticeable for multiracial students.

In using online social networking sites, even while far from home, students can maintain precollege friendships in which their identity may already be understood. In addition, the ease of communication on the Internet through instant messaging and e-mail makes maintaining supportive relationships affordable. On several occasions, I have observed students receiving validation and support from family and friends from home by e-mail. In these cases, the support has helped students persevere on campus even if they have not immediately connected with a community. In addition, using the Internet may provide students with the ability to locate other students like them, thus making their experience less isolating (Burleson, 2005).

Support services for students of color and other groups on campus are widely believed to have a positive influence on students' success. Wilds and Wilson (1998) stated, "The presence of a community with which students of color and women can identify and from which they can receive support has proven critical to the academic success of these students" (p. 58). Finding a community within the campus environment may prove challenging for multiracial students because many campuses have yet to design or implement programs and services specifically for this population (see Chapters Five and Six, this volume). Again, feeling the squeeze effect (Root, 1992), multiracial students may not feel comfortable participating in single-ethnicity support offices. In an effort to find a safe environment where they can investigate and actualize a multiracial identity, students may turn to online communities.

The Internet also provides a type of shield and may allow students who are struggling with issues of racial identity to be more comfortable exploring the ways a multiracial identity can be asserted. The importance of a safe environment for exploring identity has been noted for the gay male community. Burleson (2005) wrote, "If the fear of public exploration of sexuality is too great, the Internet allows for a safer way for those dealing with their sexual identity" (para. 3). The same may be true for students of mixed heritage who go online to connect with others who have shared common experiences instead of risking embarrassment in face-to-face situations.

The technology of the Internet and the community-building potential may already provide opportunities for solidarity and political activism among multiracial individuals. In the United States prior to the 2000 census, there was a lack of common identity or solidarity among the American multiracial population (Root, 1996). The history of multiracial people in the United States has resulted in commonly practiced assumptions, stereotypes, and misconceptions of multiracial Americans (see Chapter One, this volume). The Internet therefore may provide an opportunity for individuals to learn accurate history, replace negative stereotypes with positive images, and come together to organize around a multiracial cause.

A healthy identity is maintained by membership in an appropriate referent group (Root, 1992). It follows that multiracial individuals may be able to realize and maintain healthy identities through connections with multiracial groups online. As more and more college students create personas on social networking sites, multiracial students have the opportunity to define their identity however they wish. While some sites have a place for users to designate ethnicity (MySpace provides a drop-down menu from which to select an ethnicity from among eight monoracial groups or to choose "no answer" or "other," a fill-in-the-blank option), there is nothing to say that this portrayal must be accurate.

Root (1996) discussed the concept of "situational ethnicity" as "a natural strategy in response to the social demands of a situation for multiethnically and multiracially identified people" (p. 11). For many multiracial individuals, ethnicity takes foreground or background and changes as a natural response to stresses, social demands, or the environmental context (Root, 1996). For multiracial college students, this fluidity of identity is easily enacted through online social networking Web sites where they can post identities that may be different from how they define themselves in person. This right to change how one defines himself or herself in different contexts is one of Root's tenets (1992) in the "Bill of Rights for Multiracial Individuals." The text of this commonly cited work was found on one of the multiracial identity groups on FaceBook, as was a discussion question with the prompt, "So, what are you?" Within the context of the multiracial community, this question is loaded (see Chapters Two through Four, this volume), but it is also empowering for individuals to express themselves. As noted in Chapters Two through Four and by Root (1992, 1996), self-labeling is empowerment for multiracial individuals.

Implications for Student Affairs Practice

While promoting involvement and inclusion of multiracial students on campus should be explored, the understanding and use of new technology in programs may make outreach efforts even more successful. Student affairs practitioners should find out what students are using and become familiar with the technology so they can better assist multiracial students and meet them where they are. Professionally, not learning the technology and gaining a working knowledge is not a good option. There is clear evidence that students use technology regularly (Jones, 2005), but for the most part, these activities are not integrated into all aspects of their collegiate experience. In their study of students and information technology, Kvavik and Caruso (2005) stated, "Newer conventions such as social networking, blogging, and instant messaging, while in limited official use, are neither understood nor embraced widely by the faculty" (p. 17).

In addition to promoting knowledge acquisition by senior and veteran student affairs practitioners, student affairs graduate preparation programs need to integrate basic knowledge of technology into courses and professional outcomes. Estler (2003) stated:

> We owe students aspiring to careers in student affairs (a) the skills to function effectively in that changing world, (b) the skills to constantly acquire and

evaluate new knowledge in the face of fast paced change, and (c) knowledge and skills for leadership in assuring the centrality of student needs, in all their complexity, as technology impacts the structure and functioning of colleges and universities and with it, the student experience [para. 8].

As multicultural centers and programs seek to strengthen outreach efforts toward multiracial students, the use of technology should be in the forefront of the organizers' minds. I have observed that not all students are comfortable participating in real-time, real-life student groups on campus, nor do all students have the ability to be in the same place at the same time. These students may be more comfortable with the anonymity and community provided by an online student group through a social networking site (see Burleson, 2005). If faculty and staff are comfortable using the technology, they can participate as well, providing visible campus role models.

While online communities, blogs, wikis, and other uses of technology have many advantages, it is important to note the limitations inherent in using these tools for outreach to students. Although these tools may facilitate communication among students who would not otherwise meet in person, there are drawbacks to online methods. One significant disadvantage is the so-called digital divide between students who have readily available access to the Internet and the computers and peripherals needed to efficiently navigate it and students who do not have these resources (Galuszka, 2007). Access may be an issue for first-generation and low-income students and those from rural areas where high-speed Internet connections keep them from using Web sites to the fullest extent. Furthermore, if a student does not own a computer, sharing a roommate's computer or visiting on-campus computer labs may not only be less convenient, but also less private and therefore less safe for exploring issues of identity. Student support programs could integrate technology and provide access to computers as one solution to the digital divide and access concerns.

Another issue that is important to address with the Internet is its potential for addiction and distance between students. For those just entering the college environment, the lure to spend more time surfing than studying is great (Jones, 2002). A new student is faced with new-found freedom, less parental involvement and control, and large blocks of unstructured time (Young, 2001). These factors, combined with alienation or awkward social skills, may direct many new students to turn to the Internet instead of developing social circles on campus (Young, 2001). Bugeja (2005) called this phenomenon the "interpersonal divide": the void that develops for those who spend too much time in virtual rather than real communities.

A final concern to note here is the potential for privacy invasion and personal safety concerns. As students use social networking sites to create profiles, there are not preimposed limits to the amount of private information they can post about themselves. The inaccurate belief that only a limited community of close friends is interested or looking at a student's profile can lead to issues of cyberstalking, code of conduct violations, or other negative results (Wilson, 2007). Students new to using these sites may not be aware of the privacy controls or security issues. Student affairs administrators can help educate students to consider their online privacy as well as their personal safety (Wilson, 2007).

Conclusion

The Internet will only increase in its importance in the lives of college students. For multiracial students, the possibilities of using the Internet and technology to define identity, create community, and join together to advocate for collective issues and concerns is exciting and limitless. As student affairs practitioners seek to further support and understand the unique concerns facing this growing population on campus, effective use of technology will become increasingly important.

References

Bugeja, M. *Interpersonal Divide: The Search for Community in a Technological Age.* New York: Oxford University Press, 2005.

Burleson, D. A. "Logging On: How Technology Has Impacted the Identity Development of Gay Males." *Student Affairs Online,* 2005, 6(4). Retrieved May 31, 2007, from http://studentaffairs.com/ejournal/Fall_2005/LoggingOn.html.

Estler, S. "Designing Student Development Curriculum as Though Technology Matters." *Student Affairs Online,* 2003, 4(1). Retrieved May 31, 2007, from http://studentaffairs.com/ejournal/Winter_2003/curriculum.html.

Facebook Factsheet. 2008. Retrieved June 20, 2008, from http://www.facebook.com/press/info.php?factsheet.

Galuszka, P. "Digging Out of the Digital Divide." *Diverse Issues in Higher Education, 2007,* 24(2), 21.

Jaschick, S. "A Stand Against Wikipedia." *Inside Higher Ed,* Jan. 26, 2007. Retrieved June 30, 2007, from http://www.insidehighered.com/news/2007/01/26/wiki.

Jones, S. *The Internet Goes to College.* Sept. 15, 2002. Retrieved Mar. 24, 2008, from http://www.pewInternet.org/pds/PIP_College_Report.pdf.

Kvavik, R. B., and Caruso, J. B. "ECAR Study of Students and Information Technology: Convenience, Connection, Control, and Learning." 2005. Retrieved Mar. 20, 2008, from http://educause.edu/ir/library/pdf/ers0506/rs/ERS0506w.pdf.

Lloyd, J., Dean, L. A., and Cooper, D. L. "Students' Technology Use and Its Effects on Peer Relationships, Academic Involvement, and Healthy Lifestyles." *NASPA Journal,* 2007, 44(3). Retrieved Mar. 20, 2008, from http://publications.naspa.org/naspajournal/vol44/iss3/art6.

Matsumoto, A. "Both Yet Neither: Issues Facing Japanese American/European American Biracial and Bi-Ethnic College Students." Unpublished manuscript, University of Vermont, 1995.

"Microsoft and FaceBook Team Up for Advertising Syndication: Combination of Microsoft's and FaceBook's Consumer Assets Provides Potent Offering for Advertisers." 2006. Retrieved Mar. 20, 2008, from http://www.microsoft.com/presspass/press/2006/aug06/08-22MSFacebookPR.mspx.

Root, M.P.P. (ed.). *Racially Mixed People in America.* Thousand Oaks, Calif.: Sage, 1992.

Root, M.P.P. (ed.). *The Multiracial Experience: Racial Borders as the New Frontier.* Thousand Oaks, Calif.: Sage, 1996.

Sanford, N. *Self and Society: Social Change and Individual Development.* New York: Atherton Press, 1966.

Wilds, D., and Wilson, R. (eds.). *Minorities in Higher Education: 1997–1998.* Washington, D.C.: American Council on Education, 1998.

Wilson, S. "The Influence of Technology on College Student Values." *Student Affairs Online,* 2007, 8(3). Retrieved Mar. 20, 2008, from http://studentaffairs.com/ejournal/Fall_2007/InfluenceofTechnologyonCollegeStudentValues.html.

Young, K. "Surfing Not Studying: Dealing with Internet Addiction on Campus." *Student Affairs Online,* 2001, 2. Retrieved Aug. 31, 2007, from http://studentaffairs.com/ejournal/Winter_2001/addiction.html.

HEATHER SHEA GASSER is the interim director of the Women's Center at the University of Idaho.

8

This chapter expands the notion of biracial identity to include bicultural individuals and examines their adaptation to faculty culture in the United States.

Bicultural Faculty and Their Professional Adaptation

Michael J. Cuyjet

Most of the other chapters in this volume focus on the experience and characteristics of biracial individuals. This chapter expands the population being explored to include bicultural individuals who may differ from the definition of biracial employed elsewhere. Examples include Japanese Americans of the *Sansei* (third) generation, who are largely acculturated to the dominant culture while retaining few traditional Japanese cultural artifacts learned from older generations; American Indians who are at least one generation removed from living on a reservation and must balance the often-conflicting effects of dominant culture and the tribal culture they encounter with each visit to the reservation; and middle-class African Americans, who have always lived in predominantly White neighborhoods and attended predominantly White schools but relish the cultural customs of the Black community shared among family and friends in settings when no Whites are around. The common characteristic of the individuals on which this chapter focuses is a certain degree of acculturation to the dominant culture while retaining recognizable elements of their native culture. This experience is related but not identical to that of biracial individuals who move between cultures and heritages.

This chapter explores biculturalism in the context of higher education faculty culture. My intention is to help faculty members from minority cultures develop or enhance coping skills to better survive in the faculty culture in which they find themselves. I hope others in the university environment—students (particularly graduate students) and administrators—can sharpen their cultural coping skills as well.

NEW DIRECTIONS FOR STUDENT SERVICES, no. 123, Fall 2008 © Wiley Periodicals, Inc.
Published online in Wiley InterScience (www.interscience.wiley.com) • DOI: 10.1002/ss.288

The chapter examines nuances of faculty culture and explores why some individuals must choose to what extent they can comfortably embrace it, as well as accommodations minority faculty make to acculturate to it. I explore how people of color use their skills of bicultural and multicultural adaptation to persist and thrive in faculty communities.

Biracial and Bicultural Commonalities

Biracial and bicultural experiences are not synonymous. Some, possibly most, biracial individuals also experience bicultural influences on their lives and may well become bicultural or multicultural as a result of having a variety of developmental experiences (Fukuyama, 1999; Williams, 1999; see also Chapters Two and Three, this volume). So while many biracial people are bicultural, bicultural people are not necessarily biracial unless they also meet that definition by virtue of their parentage.

There are nonetheless some characteristics of biracialism that parallel bicultural experiences and may help in understanding a discussion of biculturalism in the academy. For example, Fukuyama (1999) wrote about bicultural individuals' experiencing a "reverse chameleon effect" that describes a circumstance in which "that which is different from the reference group will stand out" (p. 13). In predominantly White environments, bicultural individuals who identify ethnically as a minority frequently experience this effect as their nonminority colleagues project expectations on them based largely on stereotypes and assumptions about "typical" behaviors of minority group members (Thompson and Louque, 2005). Later in the chapter, I describe one common example of this phenomenon: the situation in which a minority faculty member is recruited to represent his or her racial/ethnic group on a committee.

In discussing racial identity development among biracial students, Williams (1999) suggested that some experience the "simultaneity" of being in more than one racial development stage at the same time. While bicultural faculty members who identify with an ethnic minority group have likely achieved some sense of stability in their racial identity, they may frequently be placed in situations in which they also exhibit characteristics of more than one stage of racial identity development to make sense of the conditions in which they find themselves, exhibiting what Kayes (2006) described as "the constant subtle tension between cultural identities" (p. 66). For example, a faculty member who is the only non-White person in a department would, one hopes, be at a secure enough stage in racial identity development to be able to work comfortably with White colleagues. Yet it would not be unlikely that this individual would feel compelled to manifest a version of what DuBois (1996) called the "double consciousness" of African Americans by also seeking opportunities to "immerse" in the cultural comfort of racial peers through a racially oriented faculty-staff organization or simply by choosing to establish an interdisciplinary alliance with others of the same racial/ethnic group around academic, research, or even social criteria.

Williams pointed out that this is not necessarily a regression to an earlier stage in racial identity development. Referring to minority identity development stage models (Helms, 1990), Williams (1990) used herself as an example:

> My White frame of reference is captured best by the autonomy stage and my Black frame of reference by the internalization stage (Helms, 1990). These stages refer to two very different identity processes: one for Whites and one for African Americans. Yet, I do not experience the two as split, but a fluid, seamless part of who I am. I am describing a combined consciousness that is very difficult to reconcile with existing social constructions of race and racial identity development theory [p. 34].

Although Williams was describing herself as a biracial individual, these descriptions could easily apply to an African American person who comfortably embraces both a White and a Black cultural frame of reference.

A third example of a biracial characteristic that helps explain the condition of bicultural persons in faculty settings is the phenomenon of border crossing. Root (1990) described four ways that biracial individuals resolve their identity status as being related to more than one racial group: individuals can be firmly established in both identity groups simultaneously; they can situationally shift racial foreground and background in different settings; they can claim a multiracial, central reference point; or they can establish a "home" in one identity and make occasional forays into others. Renn (2004) added a fifth option, describing students who elect to opt out of the racial definitions altogether (see Chapter Two, this volume); because of the expectations colleagues place on faculty of color, opting out is usually not a viable choice for bicultural faculty members.

Because they are socialized from the start of their membership in the faculty culture not to "deviate from the traditional academic mold" (Turner, 2002, p. 20), bicultural faculty members make choices about how they establish their faculty identity in the department similar to those described above for biracial individuals, selecting the choices that best fit the situational environment of the department's faculty culture but trying to maintain their own identity development as a member of a racial/ethnic minority (as Cross, 1995, described for African Americans). In playing into the politics of the typical faculty environment, bicultural individuals, particularly those who are seeking tenure and promotion, may learn to use one or more of these strategies in what Sands and Schuh describe as situational border crossings, in which their response to "the need to display one part of their ethnicity over another depends on where they are and with whom" (2004, p. 358).

Just as biracial individuals experience pressure from two or more cultural groups (Fukuyama, 1999; Renn, 2004; Sands and Schuh, 2004), bicultural faculty may find that pressure to conform with monocultural norms may come from either direction: other faculty of color or the dominant culture. In an example that pertains to African Americans but could easily apply to other faculty of color, Thompson and Louque (2005) explained:

> It is difficult enough for Black faculty to deal with racism, cultural insensitivity, marginalization, unfair evaluations, isolation, and so many other problems that permeate many postsecondary institutions, but when non-support from other Black faculty is added to the list, the work environment can seem even more unbearable [pp. 80–81].

This nonsupport can be a consequence of failure to conform to expected norms among Black faculty.

The dominant culture of a department's faculty can also force choices on bicultural individuals about their socialization (Tierney and Rhoads, 1993) that may prompt them not to explore their bicultural or multicultural knowledge and interests. Consider the hypothetical situation of a Latina tenure-track faculty member who wishes to study identity development among Latino/a students from urban backgrounds. If an influential member of her department's senior faculty perceives that research interest not to be "scholarly enough" and if she hopes to achieve tenure and promotion, her line of research might quickly be derailed. As Fukuyama (1999) indicated, many graduate students and faculty of color study themselves through their research. Thus, what could be a very important contribution to minority student achievement as well as an introspective examination of immense personal interest to this Latina faculty member could easily be dismissed due to the differing cultural values of colleagues.

Faculty Culture

Romantic images of higher education include assumptions that there is freedom of speech and expression punctuated by civil and intellectual discourse (Birnbaum, 1988). In such an environment, all cultures would be respected and embraced. Of course, campuses are more likely to be microcosms of society in general, with its biases and pressures for conformity. One aspect of the general society that carries over is the existence of a dominant culture within a group of faculty. For an individual who embraces the norms and customs of the dominant faculty culture, conformity is comfortable (Kayes, 2006). However, for other individuals, there are several choices: assimilation to the faculty culture, prolonged resistance and acceptance of a marginal position, or accommodation to a bicultural existence in which the individual maintains some adherence to his or her own cultural characteristics while also participating in dominant faculty culture.

One general characteristic of the faculty culture at predominantly White institutions (PWIs) that reflects a trait in the dominant culture and may conflict with typical characteristics of some minority cultures is the phenomenon of individualism (versus collectivism), in which, according to Hofstede (1991), "everyone is expected to look after himself or herself" (p. 51). As a microcosm of the general American culture, the faculty environment on many campuses epitomizes the individualistic nature of the dominant society, promoting individual achievement over group collaboration and rewarding individual accomplishments rather than celebrating collective endeavors (Birnbaum, 1988). This emphasis may have an unsettling impact on minority faculty raised in collectivist cultures such as Native American Indian tribes (Trimble and Thurman, 2002) or some Asian ethnicities (Uba, 1994), who may have to make significant adaptations to be comfortable with individualism.

Typical faculty service is about as close as faculty culture gets to a collectivist cultural structure. Although many faculty committees are collegial organizations (Birnbaum, 1988), most department faculties maintain some hierarchical structure, and new members are wise to determine the pecking order of the group and adhere to social norms (Birnbaum, 1988). Such social hierarchies are affected by cultural characteristics, so an individual raised in another cultural environment who joins a faculty group heavily influenced by the dominant culture may have to adapt his or her socialization patterns (Thompson and Louque, 2005).

Bicultural or multicultural faculty members whose heritage includes a connection to a collectivist culture may recognize that the most reinforced behaviors are derived from the dominant culture and often do not reflect the cultural characteristics of their "other" culture. For example, many Asian cultures are collectivist, such that the general welfare of the group (the family unit or social network, for example) is more important than the success of any one individual member of that group (Uba, 1994). Such collective benefits for a group rarely surface in typical U.S. faculty culture. When they do, it is often to compile the accomplishments of one faculty group to compare it to another group to see which team is the "winner," as in academic program rankings or intrainstitutional comparisons.

Many PWI faculty members who identify as having African American, Latino, or Asian American cultural backgrounds appear to have comfortably acculturated to the dominant (White) culture, while retaining their African, Latino, or Asian racial/ethnic identity. For example, in a study involving 136 African American faculty, Thompson and Louque (2005) found that a majority of study participants indicated that they felt respected, valued, and supported by their faculty colleagues. However, as this study also indicated, minority individuals who have not achieved this comfortable acculturation will undoubtedly have to make some cultural accommodation to the dominant culture that pervades the faculty workplace. Biracial faculty who have already come to terms with managing bicultural identity may have an easier experience with these same acculturation issues as they balance personal cultural identity with the dominant culture of the faculty workplace in a PWI.

Racialization of Bicultural Faculty

A significant aspect of biracial identity development (addressed in detail in Chapters Two through Four, this volume) is the pressure to select one race over another. A corresponding phenomenon that often confronts bicultural faculty members is the expectation to "represent." While there are no doubt still instances where minority faculty are asked to "speak for their race" (DeWalt, 2004), such potentially awkward situations seem to be abating. However, the "committee representation" phenomenon seems to persist. Most faculty are, as Birnbaum (1988) described, collegial organizations, in which many decisions are discussed in groups to try to achieve consensus. The faculty committee group at the program, department, school, or university level is the predominant mechanism for this dialogue.

An interesting cultural aspect of these committees is not their existence or purpose but how they are constituted. Too many times the successful "diversity" of a group in academe (such as a faculty committee) is judged by the presence of at least one representative of desired racial/ethnic groups. Tierney and Rhoads (1993) stated that "for faculty of color, additional demands relate to serving on committees where they frequently are selected to increase representation" (p. 67). They gave an example of a female American Indian professor, representing bicultural faculty members on whom "demands often are made not for the concern of the individual, but because the person represents a specific group. Each is asked to serve on many committees. Each is asked to speak for various interests even when he or she may not desire to do so" (p. 69). Thus, the bicultural faculty member who can represent a particular racial/ethnic group is called on to play that role on the committee to satisfy someone's determinant of diversity. The individual's personal worldview is often irrelevant in this situation. It is the faculty member's appearance that matters most, not his or her perspectives, attitudes, level of acculturation to the dominant culture, or stage of racial identity.

Ironically, bicultural individuals often do have something positive to contribute to these group discussions that would not be available if the group were monocultural. They can provide a worldview or perspective on life informed by experiences in a different culture and by the intersection of that culture with the dominant one. Part of the diversity training that I hope is occurring on campuses includes lessons to help faculty and staff understand that a culturally diverse committee is more than a group of people who appear different; it is a group in which the various members represent different ideas, informed by different perspectives, learned in different cultural experiences in different social environments.

NEW DIRECTIONS FOR STUDENT SERVICES • DOI: 10.1002/ss

Implications for Students

Because being a racial/ethnic minority is part of their identities, bicultural faculty can have a significant impact on biracial and monoracial students of color. This influence is generally manifested in two ways: mentoring relationships with individual students and service as advisers to student groups.

Student Mentoring. Bicultural and multicultural faculty members need to find (or help to create for themselves) an environment in which they can exercise all aspects of their multicultural identity. Yet another, almost equal important reason for these faculty members to find a comfortable environment is to allow them to serve as role models for students of racial/ethnic minority groups, including biracial students. In that capacity, they can demonstrate that success in academia includes learning how to acculturate to different cultures in both the academy and the general society without losing all characteristics of their native heritage (DeWalt, 2004). By modeling an ability to function comfortably in both native and dominant cultures, bicultural faculty members contribute to the holistic development of racial/ethnic minority students with whom they come in contact.

This lesson is particularly important for students who come to PWIs from monocultural minority environments and need assistance in navigating the nuances of a different culture at a time when they are experiencing significant developmental changes in their own racial identity (Phinney, 1989). This last point cannot be emphasized enough. Most college students, particularly those of traditional age, are experiencing a period of identity development (Evans, Forney, and Guido-DiBrito, 1998). This development is holistic, including some physical growth, psychosocial development, cognitive growth, moral development, spiritual development, gender identity, and racial identity development (Evans, Forney, and Guido-DiBrito, 1998). Role models are important in this vital growth period (see Helms, 1990; Phinney, 1989). For students who are adding acclimation to a different culture to this developmental milieu, the significance of positive role models is magnified. Bicultural faculty members who are members of racial/ethnic minority groups provide vital examples of success to students, even those with whom they may never come in contact. Biracial students who identify fully or partially as minority students in predominantly white collegiate environments would be included in this population of student beneficiaries.

Organization Advisers. A few years ago at a national convention program for new faculty, a young African American assistant professor recounted to me a story of being invited to become the faculty adviser to his institution's gospel choir, although he had no experience (and, frankly, little interest) in gospel music. This example illustrates how faculty of color are sometimes solicited to participate in activities having little connection to their primary interests and little obvious likelihood of contributing to their efforts toward tenure and promotion (Tierney and Rhoads, 1993; Watson, 2001).

NEW DIRECTIONS FOR STUDENT SERVICES • DOI: 10.1002/ss

In my opinion, such petitions for faculty service to student organizations represent a cultural conflict of sorts. If one assumes that a typical faculty culture does not give much credit for service to student organizations (at least in comparison to teaching and research-related activities), a natural reaction would be to decline any request to serve as adviser unless the students and their organization were directly related to the faculty member's own department and program. Nevertheless, faculty of color in PWI environments often recognize the needs of students of color to find role models who look like them (Watson, 2001). So the sense of cultural connectedness these faculty members feel compels participation in student-related activities such as being a faculty adviser to clubs and organizations that have little or no benefit toward the faculty member's pursuit of tenure and promotion. As an example, Tierney and Rhoads (1993) described "some of the problems Native American faculty experience because of expectations placed on them to serve as counselors and advocates for Indian students" (p. 67). Interpreting these decisions to members of the dominant culture presents both a challenge and an opportunity for bicultural faculty. The challenge derives from explaining a choice that may appear to make little sense in the calculus of faculty rewards. Watson (2001) described the service load of minority faculty identified in one study as "burdensome compared with that of both females and White males" (p. 196); thus, explaining the value of these commitments to colleagues may prove difficult. Nevertheless, serving students in this manner may offer the opportunity to teach colleagues about the tacit, and sometimes spoken, demands made on minority faculty to be available as role models to students.

Conclusion

By viewing acculturation through the lens of faculty culture at PWIs, this chapter has sought to inform the discussion of biracial people in higher education by expanding the discussion to focus on bicultural individuals, who may not be biracial but share the distinction of identifying as a member of an ethnic/racial minority. The cultural context of bicultural faculty described here may be similar enough to the situations in which biracial people often find themselves as they negotiate dominant and nondominant cultures to allow some comparisons of experiences. By assessing the cultural milieu, assessing their own racial identity, and making the necessary psychological, social, and political adjustments to the ways in which they interact with fellow faculty members, academic administrators, and students, these bicultural minority faculty members may be able to achieve success in a context that originally may not seem welcoming (Thompson and Louque, 2005). Thus, they may serve themselves by achieving success in the academy; they may serve their students, particularly minority students striving to become bicultural, as role models and mentors; they may serve their colleagues who learn new perspectives and a different world-view from them; and they may enrich the institution, which ultimately becomes a more fulfilling community because of the inclusion of divergent cultural ideas and viewpoints.

References

Birnbaum, R. *How Colleges Work: The Cybernetics of Academic Organization and Leadership*. San Francisco: Jossey-Bass, 1988.

Cross, W. E., Jr. "The Psychology of Nigrescence: Revisiting the Cross Model." In J. G. Ponterotto, J. M. Casas, L. A. Suzuki, and C. M. Alexander (eds.), *Handbook of Multicultural Counseling*. Thousand Oaks, Calif.: Sage, 1995.

DeWalt, C. S. "In the Midst of a Maze: A Need for Mentoring." In D. Cleveland (ed.), *A Long Way to Go: Conversations About Race by African American Faculty and Graduate Students*. New York: Peter Lang, 2004.

DuBois, W.E.B. *The Souls of Black Folk*. New York: Modern Library, 1996.

Evans, N., Forney, D. S., and Guido-DiBrito, F. *Student Development in College: Theory, Research, and Practice*. San Francisco: Jossey-Bass, 1998.

Fukuyama, M. A. "Personal Narrative: Growing Up Biracial." *Journal of Counseling and Development*, 1999, 77, 12–14.

Helms, J. E. *Black and White Racial Identity: Theory, Research, and Practice*. Westport, Conn.: Greenwood Press, 1990.

Hofstede, G. *Cultures and Organizations: Software of the Mind*. New York: McGraw-Hill, 1991.

Kayes, P. E. "New Paradigms for Diversifying Faculty and Staff in Higher Education: Uncovering Cultural Biases in the Search and Hiring Process." *Multicultural Education*, 2006, 14(2), 65–69.

Phinney, J. "Ethnic Identity in Adolescents and Adults: Review of Research." *Psychological Bulletin*, 1989, 108, 499–514.

Renn, K. A. *Mixed Race Students in College: The Ecology of Race, Identity, and Community*. Albany, N.Y.: SUNY Press, 2004.

Root, M. P. P. "Resolving 'Other' Status: Identity Development of Biracial Individuals." *Women and Therapy*, 1990, 9(1/2), 185–205.

Sands, N., and Schuh, J. H. "Identifying Interventions to Improve the Retention of Biracial Students: A Case Study." *Journal of College Student Retention*, 2004, 5(4), 349–363.

Thompson, G. L., and Louque, A. C. *Exposing the "Culture of Arrogance" in the Academy: A Blueprint for Increasing Black Faculty Satisfaction in Higher Education*. Sterling, Va.: Stylus, 2005.

Tierney, W. G., and Rhoads, R. A. "Enhancing Promotion, Tenure and Beyond: Faculty Socialization as a Cultural Process." *ASHE-ERIC Higher Education Report No. 6*. Washington, D.C.: ERIC Clearinghouse on Higher Education and George Washington University, 1993. (ED 368 322)

Trimble, J. E., and Thurman, P. J. "Ethnocultural Considerations and Strategies for Providing Counseling Services to Native American Indians." In P. B. Pedersen, J. G. Draguns, W. J. Lonner, and J. E. Trimble (eds.) *Counseling Across Cultures*. (5th ed.) Thousand Oaks, Calif.: Sage, 2002.

Turner, C.S.V. *Diversifying the Faculty: A Guidebook for Search Committees*. Washington, D.C.: Association of American Colleges and Universities, 2002.

Uba, L. *Asian Americans: Personality Patterns, Identity, and Mental Health*. New York: Guilford Publishing, 1994.

Watson, L. W. "The Politics of Tenure and Promotion of African American Faculty." In L. Jones (ed.), *Retaining African Americans in the Academy: Challenging Paradigms for Retaining Students, Faculty and Administrators.* Sterling, Va.: Stylus, 2001.

Williams, C. B. "Claiming a Biracial Identity: Resisting Social Constructions of Race and Culture." *Journal of Counseling and Development,* 1999, 77, 32–35.

MICHAEL J. CUYJET *is associate professor in the College Student Personnel Program in the College of Education and Human Development, and associate dean of the Graduate School at the University of Louisville.*

NEW DIRECTIONS FOR STUDENT SERVICES • DOI: 10.1002/ss

9

The perspectives of Canadians who share stories in this chapter about their mixed-race lives provide a broader context for understanding multiracial students in the United States and considering how colleges and universities in differing national and cultural contexts might best serve this growing population.

Looking North: Exploring Multiracial Experiences in a Canadian Context

Leanne Taylor

In 2002, I attended the Mixed Race Students Forum at York University in Toronto, Canada. The forum, organized by two mixed-race undergraduate students, was one of the first of its kind at the university and attracted an unexpectedly large attendance. More than one hundred students, representing a wide range of academic programs and mixed-race and multiracial backgrounds, packed into the conference room. Before the forum had even started, there was standing room only. Many in attendance sat on the floor or propped themselves up on side tables. When the forum began, its organizers explained that they wanted to open up a dialogue on the issues of mixed race among students on campus, one of Canada's largest and most racially and ethnically diverse. They hoped that a structured recognition of mixed-race experiences, which they felt were largely overlooked and misunderstood, could contribute to multiracial students' successful participation at the university.

The forum was divided into two parts. First, five students read prepared short papers or recited poetry describing their mixed-race experiences. Following the presentations, members of the larger group were invited to make comments and share their own observations and stories. Individuals outlined a host of experiences, including having to deal with inquiries into their racial background; negotiating the challenges and rewards of growing up mixed; looking racially ambiguous or not appearing mixed at all; feeling culturally isolated from certain family and community members; and being pressured to define themselves according to public perceptions of racial

NEW DIRECTIONS FOR STUDENT SERVICES, no. 123, Fall 2008 © Wiley Periodicals, Inc.
Published online in Wiley InterScience (www.interscience.wiley.com) • DOI: 10.1002/ss.289

identity and assumptions about racial classification (see also Camper, 1994; Taylor, 2000). Some situated their racially ambiguous bodies as a place of racial transcendence (Mahtani, 2005), while others, specifically those who identified as having both Black and White heritage, explained that they felt forced into what Ifekwunigwe (2001) would refer to as "compulsory black-ness," suggesting that the pressure to "choose" blackness (or one's minor-ity heritage) as an identity is often too strong to bear or resist.

Most notable in students' comments, however, was how their mixed-race identities were shaped by their experiences both at York and in Cana-dian society generally. Many perceived Canada's cultural diversity and multicultural policy as key factors shaping their varied identities, their under-standing of themselves as Canadians, and their expectations around inclu-sion and opportunity both inside and outside the university. For example, some mentioned that in a place like Canada, people should be able to claim whichever identity they want, but contradictions in the university and in multiculturalism's promise of respect for diversity, difference, and equality often prevented such claims. Students explained that despite their awareness of the many academic courses addressing racial and ethnic diversity, as well as different student-run cultural organizations (in which several claimed to participate), they often felt excluded and unacknowledged as racially mixed.

I began this chapter with a discussion of this mixed-race forum because I see its size, its mandate, and the eagerness of those in attendance as illu-minating not only common mixed-race experiences and concerns in Canada (Mahtani, 2002, 2005; Taylor, James, and Saul, 2007) but also drawing attention to their implications within the university. Despite an increasing multiracial population in Canada (Milan and Hamm, 2004), multiracial organizing is uncommon, and student services do not generally address multiracial experiences in universities. In what follows, I explore the multi-cultural context in which mixed-race people live in Canada and then dis-cuss some stories these individuals have shared about their experiences through memoirs, documentaries, and narratives. I conclude by offering some thoughts on what these experiences might suggest for higher educa-tion practices and student services in Canada and elsewhere.

Canada's Racial and Multicultural Context

While there are certainly similarities between multiracial experiences in the United States and Canada, what makes mixed race notable north of the U.S. border is its situation within a particular racial, historical, and political con-text. Canada has an international reputation as a multicultural nation that is welcoming of people who are racially and ethnically different. However, Canada's historical welcoming of differences has been questionable, espe-cially when considering its laws restricting racial and ethnic diversity. For example, Canada's colonization of aboriginal people, its treatment of the Metis, and the routine denial of land claims have limited interracial inter-

NEW DIRECTIONS FOR STUDENT SERVICES • DOI: 10.1002/ss

action between aboriginal and White populations (Dua, Razack, and Warner, 2005; Henry and Tator, 2005). Laws have also restricted the settlement of Black, Chinese, Japanese, and South Asian populations, controlling their interaction and intermarriage with Canada's European population (James, 2003; Li, 1999).

As critical racial scholars suggest, this history has contributed to an embedded structural racism that continues to have an impact on racial and ethnic interaction and the ways in which racial mixture is accepted and addressed (Bannerji, 2000; Kobayashi and Fuji Johnson, 2007). We Canadians generally perceive our country to be one of unsurpassed tolerance, freedom, and opportunity. Racism is often assumed to be behind us, upholding the color-blind idea that everyone is equal and capable of achieving the same opportunities regardless of race, ethnicity, skin color, religion, or class. Canada's particular multiculturalism policy, made into law in the 1988 Multiculturalism Act, expressly promotes and sustains these beliefs.

In fact, Canada's multicultural ideology provides the lens through which many Canadians come to engage with cultural diversity as well as understand, experience, and articulate their racial and ethnic identities (Elliot and Fleras, 1996). By placing emphasis on culture rather than racial background, multiculturalism policy claims to support individuals' choices to affiliate with any traditions or cultures they choose without discrimination. Yet rather than promote equality among its diverse population, scholars critical of multiculturalism contend that it effectively singles out individuals according to ethnicity and race by positioning some groups as "more Canadian" than others (Bannerji, 2000; Li, 1999). For example, the ideology reinforces the belief that Canada is primarily a White nation with a dual English and French heritage. "Visible minorities" (non-Whites) are the ones deemed as "having culture" and as contributing to Canada's multicultural makeup. Such cultural (largely non-White) groups are not only singled out for their particular ethnic characteristics such as food, traditions, and clothing, but those "with culture" are assumed to be homogeneous entities who come from elsewhere and share the same experiences, beliefs, and aspirations (James, 2003).

This critique is highly relevant for understanding mixed-race experiences in Canada and may provide insight into mixed-race experiences in student affairs in the United States, where multiculturalism is a prevalent ideology (see Pope, Reynolds, and Mueller, 2004). Canadian multiculturalism's focus on ethnicity and culture eschews many race-based identities, which are shaped by various forms of structural and everyday racism. As Mahtani (2002) explained, the ideology of multiculturalism creates a "burden of hyphenation where one is seen as not solely 'Canadian' but 'Canadian and fill-in-your-ethnic-background'" (p. 19). What this means is that in order for multiracial people to become visible, they must often take on identities that make sense within society's dominant cultural logic: monoracial identities (strung together with hyphens such as Jamaican-Canadian, Chinese-Pakistani-Canadian, and so on). However, the Canadian tendency to use cultural hyphens to identify who is Canadian and who is not overlooks the complexity of mixed-race identities, which are often situated outside or between racial and ethnic categories (Mahtani, 2002). As the students at the forum expressed, this situation can reinforce mixed-race experiences of displacement and misrecognition (Taylor and others, 2007). Thus, the more that mixed-race identities challenge the norms of what is understood as "Canadian," the more mixed-race people will be positioned as doubly different, doubly strange, and doubly foreign (Mahtani, 2002).

It is in this context of multiculturalism and a presumed equality of opportunity that we can interpret many mixed-race experiences in Canada and at Canadian universities. While there has been considerably less empirical research on mixed race in Canadian contexts compared to the United States, and even less exploration of such experiences in educational spaces, this research is growing. There are parallels between the United States and Canada, but here, I want to draw attention to some experiences that speak to Canadian contexts. The stories that follow offer further insight into how some mixed-race individuals experience life in Canada, negotiate racism in their lives, and articulate their identities. These insights may be useful in understanding mixed-race Canadian college students and broadening perspectives on student experiences in the United States. My discussion is not a suggestion that there is a singular mixed-race experience in Canada, but that these perspectives say something significant about the complexity of such experiences and draw attention to the role educators might play in addressing them.

Exploring Mixed Race Experiences in Canada

In his memoir *Black Berry Sweet Juice: On Being Black and White in Canada*, Lawrence Hill asked: "What does it mean to be black and white in Canada?" (2001, p. 7). Reflecting on his experiences, he explained that the racism and feelings of exclusion people of color might commonly feel in the United States can take a different form in Canada. In Canada, he wrote, "Racism is like a fleet-footed bedbug that runs for cover under a sweet-smelling duvet stuffed with politeness and tolerance for multiculturalism" (p. 155). As a result, "Canadians are quick to point out what we of mixed race are not—we are not white, and we are not black—but they don't tell us what we are. . . . This is the quintessential Canada: the True North, Proud, and Vague" (p. 228).

Although Hill and his family often visited his Black cousins and relatives in the United Sates, he noted that growing up in Canada was different. In the United States, he was assumed to be Black, was expected to participate in Black-identified activities, and was even admonished for his love of squash, a so-called White sport. In Canada, "Unlike my cousins, I had at least some room to concoct my own identity, declare it, test it out, see how it flew out there in my world. This, I think, is what still defines Canada today for a mixed-race person. There is some wiggle room" (2001, p. 229).

NEW DIRECTIONS FOR STUDENT SERVICES • DOI: 10.1002/ss

But, as Hill warned, "Canadians may let you wiggle occasionally, but you're going to have to scratch and claw like mad to get anywhere discernibly new" (2001, p. 229).

Camille Hernandez-Ramdwar offered further insight into some of the limits imposed on mixed-race identity. She explained that ultimately "you must choose an identity, a racialized community, a moniker to get you through some door, even if you're not entirely welcome in the world it opens into" (2001, p. 118). She explained that while growing up, she would offer elaborate explanations about her racial and ethnic background to account for her father's mixed Indian and Spanish origins and his homeland of Trinidad, as well as her mother's White Ukrainian "Canadianness" and her home town of "small-town Manitoba." Although these definitions were sufficient for her and her family while growing up, she quickly learned that "to my peers my dark skin placed me in other categories: Nigger, Darkie, Paki, Injun. I would come home crying—'They called me nigger!'" (p. 117).

As Hernandez-Ramdwar entered into academic life, she was further reminded that mixed race was not always valued as an identity in and of itself, nor did being mixed race shield her from experiencing racism both inside and outside school. Rather, she explained that racially mixed people must become

> Black, South Asian, Asian, Aboriginal and then make attempts to inject our multiplicity into arenas where purity and loyalty and allegiance demand clear-cut and defined boundaries. In the event that we are allowed to name ourselves as "mixed-race" we must append a further definer to fit within the representative festival, history month, panel, conference, course, work-shop. Therefore, one becomes Black Mixed-Race or Asian Mixed-Race or Caribbean Mixed-Race or a Mixed-Race woman—something plus mixedness. As if the mix itself weren't enough [p. 118].

Hernandez-Ramdwar's experiences made her aware of the inevitability of racism in Canada—a racism her parents tried hard to deny and ignore. Thus, while her parents encouraged her to assert her mixed heritage while growing up, she felt that they were ultimately unable to recognize challenges she faced as racially mixed. In addition, her personal interviews with mixed-race students in Toronto reveal a desire for a safe space that can seem elusive in contexts that continue to ignore those who do not fit. As a graduate student interacting with academics, her own sense of safety was often denied as she was subjected to scrutiny and suspicion by those who "feel threatened by the presence of mixed-race people in their circle" (p. 121).

Anne Marie Nakagawa's documentary *Between: Living in the Hyphen* (2005) and Shanti Thakur's (1994) documentary *Domino* reveal additional struggles and contradictions. In Nakagawa's film, interviewees explain how "multiculturalism was never really designed to imagine me." Their "in-betweenness" is put on trial and determined to be culturally different, confusing, and "un-Canadian." Karina Vernon, an interviewee who identifies as Black, South Asian, and British, interprets questions such as, "Where are you from?" as revoking her claims to Canadianness. She also describes feeling phony and inauthentic among racial and ethnic groups. Significant in each of these documentaries are individuals' feelings of isolation, invisibility, and nonbelonging, bolstered by the fact that many saw few outlets (at home, with friends, or at school) to which they could turn and share their experiences. As Thakur (1994) described, mixed-race people can become "cultural brokers" who are often overlooked within families. She explains that because they are commonly "the minority within the minority" (p. 349), they are even more vulnerable to internalizing "the racism that seeps into our consciousness: through the media, school, the extended family, our peers etc." (p. 346).

Mixed-race narratives like these show that in this multicultural context, racism is hidden and covert, but very real for those who face it in multiple aspects of their lives. They also point to how mixed-race experiences are often overlooked in Canada and within its institutional structures. Given that universities do not operate in a vacuum but reflect society's issues and values, the implications for higher education are significant.

Rethinking Mixed-Race and Student Services in Canada

Statistics Canada (Bélanger and Malenfant, 2005) projected that by 2017, one-fifth of Canada's population will identify as belonging to a visible minority group. Many universities, particularly those in urban centers, have attempted to address such demographic shifts by establishing more inclusive policies and diversifying course content, enrollment, and faculty hiring processes (James, 2003; Khan and Pavlich, 2000). The Canadian Association of College and University Student Services (1999) further advocates for students and faculty in tertiary institutions. Part of its mandate is to "strive to educate, support, regulate, respond, and promote activities that protect the rights and responsibilities of students as members of the campus community" (p. 35). As "advocates for students," association members are expected to use "their knowledge and expertise of student development principles to support and foster the importance of the total growth of the individual through programs and services that facilitate students' psychological, social, ethical, cultural and spiritual development" and "promote the importance of diversity on our campuses" (p. 35). However, such initiatives and associations have not addressed the growing numbers of students and faculty claiming multiple racial and ethnic backgrounds. Nor do they acknowledge or explore the ways in which these shifts present new challenges for the university environment and the way issues of diversity and equity should subsequently be addressed.

Research continually finds that universities are integral in maintaining and developing racial and ethnic identities and creating involved citizens (Khan and Pavlich, 2000; Razack, 1999). Students' experiences outside the classroom are crucial to the learning process—to what happens inside the classroom and to what they come to expect from their education (Henry and Tator, 2005; James, 2003; Razack, 1999). Although Canadian universities claim to be doing their job by upholding principles of multiculturalism, the mixed-race students at York (and those I have mentioned) tell a different story. They express that their experiences of in-betweenness, invisibility, and lack of support are overlooked and misunderstood. For them, the university, like multiculturalism, conflates racial and ethnic intergroup and intragroup differences and fails to accommodate many of their complex needs, issues, and identities.

These examples, though merely scratching the surface of a complicated set of experiences, are important for student services professionals and educators in both the United States and Canada who are interested in meeting the needs of increasingly diverse student populations. For one, they strengthen the call for further research into mixed-race experiences that would give insight into how students' identities and experiences factor into their personal learning objectives. This is a notable prerequisite for planning university curricula, programs, and services and also for cultivating supportive campus environments that enhance student learning and development (Renn, 2004).

More specifically, and as noted throughout this volume, student service providers must direct their attention toward the range of experiences and backgrounds of their students. This shift includes making decisions that not only recognize but also counter assumptions reinforced by broader society and within multicultural frameworks, including assumptions that institutions of higher education are immune to reproducing inequitable social structures and ideologies (Lee and Lutz, 2005). If universities and those working within them are to be truly committed to supporting students and creating positive learning environments, then they will have to resist replicating social norms that hyphenate, homogenize, overlook, and thus exclude multiracial differences, needs, and interests. A commitment to multiculturalism is not sufficient. The point is not that we merely nurture identities and pay homage to a set of broad but separate differences. Rather, the hope is that when universities and educators commit to understanding and supporting differences, they acknowledge the relationship between and across all differences and groups on their campuses.

Student services would do well to include more forums on mixed-race issues and develop courses and curriculum that address the growing population of mixed-race students and their complex relationships with family, community, and peers. Attention to whether cultural forums and programs on campus are inclusive of perspectives of mixture and the interrelationship between groups could be also fruitful. Furthermore, what role can and should students play in this process? Students cannot be charged with the sole responsibility of addressing these issues, as was the case for the York forum. What, then, should be the role of organizations such as the Canadian Association of College and University Student Services, among others?

Because Canadian approaches to diversity are frequently framed within a multicultural framework that can overlook mixture and cross-over (Bannerji, 2000) and also position racism as an individual problem that can hide the power of structural influences (Elliott and Fleras, 1996; Li, 1999), there has been minimal institutional support and services for issues of mixed race. Consequently, the York forum has remained the only one of its kind at the school to date. Deeper involvement by student services might help make such initiatives sustainable and effective across time.

It warrants asking that if multiracial students, whose numbers are increasing quickly, cannot see themselves reflected in university curriculum and services, then whose knowledge and interests are being reproduced? It is imperative that faculty, student services providers, students, and administrators alike be involved in the process of diversifying universities in a way that will account for a range of differences such as mixed race. Until such a shift is made, it is likely that many mixed-race students will continue to feel positioned on the borders of inclusion.

References

Bannerji, H. *The Dark Side of the Nation: Essays on Multiculturalism, Nationalism and Gender.* Toronto: Canadian Scholars' Press, 2000.

Bélanger, A., and Malenfant, E. C. *Population Projections of Visible Minority Groups, Canada, Provinces and Regions: 2001–2017.* Ottawa, Ontario: Statistics Canada, 2005.

Camper, C. (ed.). *Miscegenation Blues: Voices of Mixed Race Women.* Toronto: Sister Vision Press, 1994.

Canadian Association of College and University Student Services. *Policy and Procedures Manual,* revised. 1999. Retrieved Mar. 22, 2008, from http://www.cacuss.ca/files/cacuss/policymanual.pdf.

Dua, E., Razack, N., and Warner, J. N. (eds.). *Social Justice: A Journal of Crime, Conflict, and World Order,* 2005, 32 (entire issue 4).

Elliott, J. L., and Fleras, A. *Unequal Relations: An Introduction to Race and Ethnic Dynamics in Canada.* (2nd ed.) Upper Saddle River, N.J.: Prentice Hall, 1996.

Henry, F., and Tator, C. *The Colour of Democracy: Racism in Canadian Society.* (3rd ed.) Toronto: Thomson Nelson, 2005.

Hernandez-Ramdwar, C. "The Elusive and Illusionary: Identifying of Me, Not by Me." In C. E. James and A. Shadd (eds.), *Talking About Identity: Encounters in Race, Ethnicity and Language.* Toronto: Between the Lines, 2001.

Hill, L. *Black Berry Sweet Juice: On Being Black and White in Canada.* Toronto: HarperCollins Canada, 2001.

Ifekwunigwe, J. "Re-membering 'Race': On Gender, 'Mixed Race' and Family in the English-African Diaspora." In D. Parker and M. Song (eds.), *Rethinking "Mixed Race."* London: Pluto Press, 2001.

James, C. E. *Seeing Ourselves: Exploring Race, Ethnicity and Culture.* Toronto: Thompson Publishing, 2003.

Khan, S., and Pavlich, D. *Academic Freedom and the Inclusive University.* Vancouver: UBC Press, 2000.

Kobayashi, A., and Johnson, G. F. "Introduction." In G. F. Johnson and R. Enomoto (eds.), *Race, Racialization, and Antiracism in Canada and Beyond.* Toronto: University of Toronto Press, 2007.

Lee, J., and Lutz, J. (eds.). *Situating "Race" and Racisms in Space, Time, and Theory: Critical Essays for Activists and Scholars.* Canada: McGill–Queens University Press, 2005.

Li, P. *The Chinese in Canada.* (2nd ed.) New York: Oxford University Press, 1998.

Li, P. "The Multiculturalism Debate." In P. S. Li (ed.), *Race and Ethnic Relations in Canada.* (2nd ed.) New York: Oxford University Press, 1999.

Mahtani, M. "Interrogating the Hyphen-Nation: Canadian Multicultural policy and 'Mixed-Race' Identities." *Social Identities* 2002, 8(1), 67–90.

Mahtani, M. "Mixed Metaphors: Positioning 'Mixed Race' Identity." In J. Lee and J. Lutz (eds.), *Situating "Race" and Racisms in Space, Time, and Theory: Critical Essays for Activists and Scholars.* Canada: McGill–Queens University Press, 2005.

Milan, A., and Hamm, B. "Mixed Unions." *Canadian Social Trends*, no. 73, 2004, 2–6.

Nakagawa, A. M. *Between: Living in the Hyphen.* Montreal: National Film Board of Canada, 2005. DVD.

Pope, R. L., Reynolds, A. L., and Mueller, J. A. *Multicultural Competence in Student Affairs.* San Francisco: Jossey-Bass, 2004.

Razack, S. *Looking White People in the Eye: Gender, Race, and Culture in the Courtrooms and Classrooms.* Toronto: University of Toronto Press, 1999.

Renn, K. *Mixed Race Students in College. The Ecology of Race, Identity, and Community on Campus.* Albany, N.Y.: SUNY Press, 2004.

Taylor, L. "Black, White, Beige, Other? Memories of Growing Up Different." In C. E. James (ed.), *Experiencing Difference.* Halifax: Fernwood, 2000.

Taylor, L., James, C. E., and Saul, R. "Who Belongs? Exploring Race and Racialization in Canada." In G. F. Johnson and R. Enomoto (eds.), *Race, Racialization, and Antiracism in Canada and Beyond.* Toronto: University of Toronto Press, 2007.

Thakur, S. "Domino: Filming Stories of Interracial People." In C. Camper (ed.), *Miscegenation Blues: Voices of Mixed Race Women.* Toronto: Sister Vision Press, 1994.

LEANNE TAYLOR is completing her doctorate in the Faculty of Education at York University, Toronto, Canada.

10

This chapter describes how the emerging multiracial student population is influencing policy, procedures, and programs within higher education in the United States.

Student Affairs and Higher Education Policy Issues Related to Multiracial Students

Angela Kellogg, Amanda Suniti Niskodé

Race-based policies and programs for higher education were mainly based on the needs and interests of monoracial students. Until recently, federal policies as well as campus practices have reflected this mind-set. This chapter provides an overview of U.S. national policy regarding racial data collection and reporting, including implications for campuses. It also discusses how to expand thinking beyond monoracial categories through improving the infrastructure of programs and services on campus and reexamining affirmative action policies to ensure the consideration of multiracial students.

Racial and Ethnic Data Collection and Reporting

In order to serve multiracial students effectively, it is imperative that student affairs professionals understand the history and current status of national policy regarding racial identification and its impact on how campuses collect and maintain data on race and ethnicity.

Status of National Policy. Policy surrounding racial classification is governed by Statistical Directive 15 of the U.S. Office of Management and Budget (OMB) (Fernandez, 1996). The purpose of this directive is to ensure that all federal agencies, such as schools, the Social Security Administration, and the Bureau of the Census, report data in consistent categories. The directive defined four racial categories—White, Black, Asian/Pacific Islander,

NEW DIRECTIONS FOR STUDENT SERVICES, no. 123, Fall 2008 © Wiley Periodicals, Inc.
Published online in Wiley InterScience (www.interscience.wiley.com) • DOI: 10.1002/ss.290

American Indian/Alaskan Native—and required that each person be counted in only one of these groups, plus ethnicity of Hispanic Origin or Not Hispanic Origin. Although some federal agencies provided an option for individuals to check more than one box or mark "other," they still had to report the data in the designated monoracial categories.

A major change occurred in 1997 when the OMB revised Statistical Directive 15, expanding to five racial categories (American Indian/Alaska Native, Asian, Black/African American, Native Hawaiian or Other Pacific Islander, White) and for the first time requiring federal agencies to offer the option to choose more than one racial category. This policy change allowed Americans to classify themselves as belonging to multiple racial categories on the 2000 U.S. Census. This was a major step for multiracial people, because in the past they were forced to deny an aspect of their identity. According to Douglass (2000),

> What has been dismantled by this shift in public policy is the mythical notion that race is fixed rather than fluid, or that any governmental agency's perception of racial identity takes priority over an individual's right to self-identify. The American people will finally be able to display a full range of single and multiple race responses reflecting the truly diverse fabric of our current and historical roots [para. 2].

More than 6.8 million people indicated more than one racial category on the 2000 census (Jones and Smith, 2001). This group included over 2.8 million people under the age of eighteen, many of whom will be college bound in the near future.

The OMB mandated that federal agencies implement the policy changes by January 1, 2003. Yet the Department of Education (DOE) did not immediately comply (Kean, 2006). Many higher education governing organizations agreed that postsecondary institutions would have to change data collection methods to be consistent with OMB, but felt that institutions would need several years to administer the changes due to the extensive resources necessary to overhaul existing databases. This process was delayed because college officials were waiting for definitive guidelines from the National Center for Educational Statistics (NCES) before making changes. In 2002, NCES had still not told institutions how to report race and ethnicity information to the Integrated Postsecondary Education Data System, the primary data collection program for NCES. Thus, NCES recommended that institutions wait until they received further instructions (Renn and Lunceford, 2004).

In 2007, the DOE issued "Final Guidance on Maintaining, Collecting and Reporting Data on Racial and Ethnic Data," which would permit students to indicate two or more races. The guidance requires the use of a two-step format for data collection. Students will first indicate if they are of Hispanic/Latino origin, whatever their race. Next they will select one or more of the following five categories: American Indian or Alaskan native;

Asian; Black or African American; native Hawaiian or other Pacific Islander; and White. Anyone who has selected more than one box will be reported to the DOE in a "two or more races" category.

Although this change seemed like a step in the right direction, the policy has created a few challenges. There are fears that single-identity minority groups will see a decrease in the enrollment numbers of their respective population (Jaschik, 2006). For example, a White and Asian American student who had previously checked the "Asian American" box in the past might now check both Asian and White, placing her in the "two or more races" category instead of the Asian category. Also, some organizations, such as the MAVIN Foundation, have expressed concern with the guidelines because the "two or more races" category obscures the unique racial makeup of individuals. The education manager of the MAVIN Foundation, Alfredo J. Padilla, stated, "Someone who indicated he is American Indian and Black would be grouped in the same multiracial category as someone who is Native Hawaiian and White. It makes the assumption that everyone within that category is the same" (Kean, 2006, para. 15).

Despite these challenges, the changes present potential opportunities for educational institutions, such as providing a more accurate representation of the student population on campus, as well as specific information on various outcomes and experiences of multiracial students. The Final Guidance requires educational institutions to implement the changes by fall 2010 and report data in this format for the 2010–2011 school year; however, institutions are encouraged to begin immediately if feasible.

Implications for Campuses. There is wide variation in how colleges and universities in the United States collect racial and ethnic data for students who identify with more than one race (Padilla and Kelley, 2005). Most institutional forms contain some variation on the five traditional racial/ethnic categories; however, beyond this basic structure, many differences exist. Students might be asked to check one box; select a "multiracial" or equivalent category; mark multiple races; or choose an "other" designation and further specify their race or ethnicity. In a 2005 survey of 298 U.S. colleges and universities, only 27 percent offered students an option to identify their multiracial heritage on admissions applications, and only 3 percent consistently retained data on a student's specific racial or ethnic heritage (Padilla and Kelley, 2005).

The need for colleges to collect more precise data on the racial and ethnic backgrounds of their students is becoming increasingly evident. Data on race and ethnicity are used for a number of important purposes in higher education, such as tracking access, retention, and equity. Yet current classification systems are inadequate to reflect the changing student population. An increasing number of college students are refusing to identify their race at all on admissions applications. The number of students in higher education for whom race is unknown doubled between 1991 and 2001 to 938,000, or 6 percent of all students, and increased further to 1.1 million in 2004 (Jaschik, 2006). Furthermore, many multiracial college students

NEW DIRECTIONS FOR STUDENT SERVICES • DOI: 10.1002/ss

object to being forced to mark one box to reflect their heritage and want opportunities to identify themselves in ways compatible with their own understanding of their racial identity (Renn, 2004).

Appropriate data collection and reporting is essential to ensure an accurate picture of student diversity and meet the needs of the growing number of multiracial students. The U.S. Department of Education's Guidance (2007) will undoubtedly change the ways many institutions collect and report information about students' race and ethnicity on admissions and other institutional forms. At a minimum, institutions will be required to allow students to pick multiple boxes and report those students in a new "two or more races" category. Yet there is latitude for institutions to collect additional data or to run multiple data analyses in order better to reflect students' racial and ethnic backgrounds. For instance, institutions are encouraged to disaggregate racial and ethnic data from the "two or more races" category and report the number of students who identify with specific mixed-heritage combinations (U.S. Department of Education, 2007; Padilla and Kelley, 2005). The report "One Box Is Not Enough" provided examples of several institutions, such as the University of Washington and Providence College, that encode and present data on race and ethnicity to account for multiracial students (Padilla and Kelley, 2005).

In higher education, the ability to compare data within and across institutions is essential in analyzing trends and understanding a number of outcomes in postsecondary education (Renn and Lunceford, 2004). Thus, methods must be developed to link the new data with data collected before the option of multiple racial/ethnic categories, a process referred to as bridging. Administrators and staff should familiarize themselves with possible bridging techniques, such as those included in OMB's 2001 Provisional Guidance on the Implementation of the 1997 Standards for Federal Data on Race and Ethnicity, and develop a set of guiding principles and decision rules for this process. The DOE requires that bridging methods are documented and available for review if needed. The Final Guidance also recommends that institutions allow all current students and staff the opportunity to reidentify their race and ethnicity using the categories outlined in the Final Guidance.

In addition, institutions must clearly state how the data are encoded, including how and when racial categories are collapsed. Some multiracial students have expressed concern that if they check more than one category, institutions will be required to report data in monoracial categories and therefore will "choose" students' race for them (Kellogg, 2006). It is important that students are notified how the data will be aggregated, so that they can make an informed decision on how to respond (Kellogg, 2006). Furthermore, institutions should be aware of research on multiracial persons— such as the fluidity of multiracial identity and the discrepancy between individual and social identity—that might complicate data collection and interpretation (Leong, 2006; Renn and Lunceford, 2004).

It is apparent that significant changes are in store regarding the policies and procedures for collecting and reporting racial and ethnic data. These changes are long overdue and mark positive progress in demonstrating that race and ethnicity do not fit neatly into distinct categories. Yet these revisions will not happen overnight. Data collection and reporting are complex processes that must be coordinated across various campus offices (Renn and Lunceford, 2004) such as institutional research, admissions, registrar, and information technology. Inevitably changes will involve modifications to data systems, preparation of new forms, and staff training (U.S. Department of Education, 2007). It is imperative that institutions develop implementation plans that are effective and useful for students, the campus, and the larger data community. These changes must also extend beyond the institutional setting to agencies, researchers, and others who collect and maintain data on system, regional, and national levels. Doing so will give students the opportunity to reflect their heritage, provide institutions with a better representation of the composition of student populations, and offer valuable information on multiracial students' experiences in college.

Programs and Policies: Expanding the Monoracial Focus

Like much of the rest of society, higher education institutions were created with monoracial populations in mind. Broadening the focus of programs and policies to serve multiracial students more effectively is a challenge for the 21st century.

Campus Programs and Services. Many institutions' operations are still structured around the traditional paradigm of monoracial categories. Campus support offices for students of color are often organized around Black, Asian, Hispanic/Latino, and Native American issues. Similarly, student organizations are typically centered on individual racial/ethnic groups.

Colleges and universities need to take steps to ensure that the organizational structure supports the needs of multiracial students. Students and educators must create a safe and welcoming climate for multiracial students in existing monoracial organizations, as well as support the growing number of organizations for multiracial students. While the issues surrounding student services and student organizations are discussed in Chapters Five and Six of this volume, it is important to recognize that institutional policies can have an impact on the ways in which multiracial students are engaged in the campus environment. Educators should consider the message that campus policies and practices (formal and informal) convey about how multi-racial students are valued (Renn, 2004). Consider the following topics:

• *Recruitment.* Numerous institutions use designated minority recruiters to attract different racial groups to their campus (Flanagan, Howard, and

Whitla, 2004). However, such a practice might exclude students who identify themselves as multiracial unless someone is also assigned to this population. Educators need to consider if such policies and other recruitment strategies portray diversity only in terms of monoracial categories.

- *Assumptions.* It is vital that as colleges and university leaders reorganize their infrastructure to support multiracial students, they check their own assumptions about what it means to be multiracial. Many multiracial students react negatively when others mistakenly assume their racial identity (Sands and Schuh, 2003). Thus, when attempting to establish diverse representation on a campus committee, for example, leaders should not assume racial identities based on students' physical appearance or name.

- *Curriculum.* The monoracial focus can also be expanded within the classroom, which could have implications for budgets, curricula, and course offerings. Although cultural studies courses and academic programs, such as Asian American or Native American studies, are typically devoted to monoracial groups, some institutions already support courses and programs devoted to multiracial studies. For example, a growing number of classes are focused on multiracial issues, such as "The Anthropology of Mixed Race" at Grinnell College and "People of Mixed Racial Descent" at the University of California, Berkeley. Such courses can help students challenge fixed and rigid racial categories and provide the language, theory, and cognitive tools to understand the complexity of race (Renn, 2004).

Now more than ever before multiracial students and professionals are speaking up about the importance of their identity. Many are united to establish policies, programs, and services on campus that will enhance their experience through organizations such as the American College Personnel Association's Multiracial Network, the MAVIN Foundation, and the Mixed Heritage Center. However, educators need not wait for the multiracial community to challenge the status quo. Instead they can work to empower this population by reconceptualizing diversity to include multiracial issues, which may also improve the campus climate and learning opportunities for everyone (Gurin, Dey, Gurin, and Hurtado, 2004).

Affirmative Action. Affirmative action continues to be an ongoing debate in the United States, with much attention directed toward higher education. In 2003, the U.S. Supreme Court upheld the University of Michigan Law School's admissions policy, ruling that diversity can serve as a "compelling interest" and that colleges and universities can consider race and ethnicity in admissions decisions (*Grutter* v. *Bollinger*, 2003). In its decision, the Court acknowledged the educational benefits of a diverse student body, a position supported by substantial research indicating that students' experiences with racial and ethnic diversity enhance numerous learning and democracy outcomes and contribute to a richer learning environment for all students (Gurin, Dey, Gurin, and Hurtado, 2004). Although the court decision provided long-awaited guidance on the status of affirmative action in higher education, it also left many unanswered questions. For example, the U.S. Court of Appeals Sixth District, which upheld the law school's admissions policy, ignored many difficult issues inherent in racial categorization and disregarded the increasing prevalence of multiracial people in the United States (Skrentny, 2002).

As changes in racial and ethnic reporting allow students to check more than one box, higher education institutions will increasingly face the issue of how to consider multiracial students under current affirmative action policies. Changes to the collection and reporting of racial and ethnic data may also complicate policy enforcement, since these numbers are used to measure the effectiveness of affirmative action (Rosin, 1994). Perhaps the most sensitive area lies in the admissions process, where reviewers must decide how to evaluate applications from multiracial applicants for the purposes of affirmative action (Leong, 2006). In addition, institutions will need to address the issue of how to consider multiracial students for scholarships designated for students from certain heritage groups. For instance, would a student who is one-quarter Black qualify for a scholarship targeted for African American students? Would this student be considered the same as a monoracial student in admissions decisions?

There are no easy answers to these questions. Current practice appears to indicate that most higher education institutions consider multiracial students as students of color (Padilla and Kelley, 2005). Indeed, some people feel that it makes sense to include multiracial persons in affirmative action policies since many multiracial people have been subject to racism and discrimination (Fernandez, 1996). Some advocacy groups fear that allowing students to identify as multiracial will cause minority racial groups to lose benefits, and thus undermine the enforcement of civil rights laws (Schmidt, 1997). Conversely, concerns exist that including multiracial students with monoracial groups for the purpose of affirmative action classification displays insensitivity to multiracial students' right to self-determination and potentially inflates the number of students in higher education who identify with these communities (Leong, 2006).

In the light of these issues, colleges and universities must address how they will evaluate multiracial students in the context of affirmative action programs. Administrators should review their procedures for admissions, financial aid, employment, and other programs to discuss how multiracial students will be considered and to ensure that the intended goals of affirmative action are met. There is little direction for institutions in this area, although the OMB (2000) did provide guidance for how federal agencies should aggregate and allocate multiple race data for civil rights monitoring and enforcement. In the admissions arena, many institutions are moving toward a comprehensive review of applications as a result of the *Grutter* (2003) decision, which held that admissions programs must be "narrowly tailored" and involve an "individualized and holistic review" of each applicant's file. Although this process will undoubtedly be complicated and time-consuming, it may also give institutions latitude to look "beyond the boxes" and allow multiracial applicants to share aspects of their background and experiences that they believe are relevant and contribute to diversity on campus (Leong, 2006).

As the multiracial population on college campuses grows, so will the debate about who qualifies—and who does not—under affirmative action policies. Skrentny (2002) stated, "Mixed-race people are enough of a force that they have changed how they are counted on the census. For affirmative action to survive, it needs a more-rigorous legal foundation for the policy than the Grutter decision provides" (p. B20). However, colleges and universities cannot necessarily wait until these issues are more clearly defined within the legal system. There is too much at stake. As institutions seek to implement affirmative action policies, they must take changing demographics into account and recognize the many ways in which multiracial students may enrich campus diversity.

Conclusion

As the policy context in higher education shifts toward a greater recognition of multiracial students, it is important that institutions proceed carefully. These issues involve not only logistical changes, such as revisions to institutional forms, but personal identities and political stakes as well (Renn and Lunceford, 2004). Campus officials need to be sensitive to emotions surrounding issues of race and identity and engage members of the campus community in dialogue at every stage. It is also important to recognize the potential impact of policy changes—such as who benefits and who might be negatively affected—and to plan for the investment of time and money that changes may require. It is critical to include students in these discussions. Already, many multiracial students have become advocates for policy changes at the institutional and national levels (Hamako, 2005). There is an opportunity to educate students about multiracial issues and teach them how to affect policy and create change.

In addition, assessment and future research are necessary. As with any other policy, it is imperative that institutional leaders engage in assessment and use the data to inform and refine future policy. Also, there is scant literature and empirical research on topics related to multiracial persons and higher education policy, despite the growing prominence of these issues (Leong, 2006). Research could be conducted to ascertain how multiracial students are considered in affirmative action and within the institutional structure (offices, programs, and organizations), as well as how institutions are aggregating and reporting racial and ethnic data following the DOE Guidance.

It is unknown at this time what the future holds regarding multiracial students in the context of higher education policy. Yet changes are inevitable, as the coming years will likely bring new issues to the forefront. Certainly, as Renn (2004) stated, "There are no easy formulas for transforming higher education policy and practice better to reflect and meet the needs of an increasing number of mixed race students" (p. 252). Yet institutions must address policies and programs to consider the needs of this growing population and prepare campus communities for the rapidly changing landscape in which students will live and learn.

References

Douglass, R. E. *Upgrading America's Conversations on Race: The Multi-Race Option for Census 2000.* 2000. Retrieved Aug. 16, 2007, from http://www.ameasite.org/census/upgrade2k.asp.

Fernandez, C. A. "Government Classification of Multiracial/Multiethnic People." In M.P.P. Root (ed.), *The Multiracial Experience: Racial Borders as the New Frontier.* Thousand Oaks, Calif.: Sage, 1996.

Flanagan, E., Howard, C., and Whitla, D. *Recruitment and Admissions Strategies for Diversifying the Student Body.* Cambridge, Mass.: Harvard University, School of Education, 2004.

Grutter v. Bollinger, 539 U.S. 306 (2003).

Gurin, P., Dey, E., Gurin, G., and Hurtado, S. "The Educational Value of Diversity." In P. Gurin, J. S. Lehman, and E. Lewis (eds.), *Defending Diversity: Affirmative Action at the University of Michigan.* Ann Arbor: University of Michigan Press, 2004.

Hamako, E. "For the Movement: Community Education Supporting Multiracial Organizing." *Equity and Excellence in Education,* 2005, *38,* 145–154.

Jaschik, S. "An End to Picking One Box." *Inside Higher Ed,* Aug. 8, 2006. Retrieved Aug. 1, 2007, from http://www.insidehighered.com/news/2006/08/08/race.

Jones, N. A., and Smith, A. S. "The Two or More Races Population: 2000." Washington, D.C.: U.S. Census Bureau, 2001.

Kean, S. "Education Department May Give Students More Options in Identifying Their Race." *Chronicle of Higher Education,* Sept. 1, 2006. Retrieved Aug. 1, 2007, from http://chronicle.com/weekly/v53/i02/02a04602.htm.

Kellogg, A. "Exploring Critical Incidents in the Racial Identity of Multiracial College Students." Unpublished doctoral dissertation, University of Iowa, 2006.

Leong, N. "Multiracial Identity and Affirmative Action." Berkeley Electronic Press, 2006. Retrieved May 2, 2007, from http://law.bepress.com/expresso/eps/1126.

Padilla, A., and Kelley, M. *One Box Isn't Enough: An Analysis of How U.S. Colleges and Universities Classify Mixed Heritage Students.* 2005. Retrieved Aug. 15, 2007, from http://www.mavinfoundation.org/projects/obie_report_110905.pdf.

Renn, K. A. *Mixed Race Students in College: The Ecology of Race, Identity and Community on Campus,* Albany, N.Y.: SUNY Press, 2004.

Renn, K. A., and Lunceford, C. J. "Because the Numbers Matter: Transforming Postsecondary Education Data on Student Race and Ethnicity to Meet the Challenges of a Changing Nation." *Education Policy,* 2004, *18*(5), 752–783.

Rosin, H. "Boxed In." *New Republic,* 1994, *210*(1), 12.

Sands, N., and Schuh, J. H. "Identifying Interventions to Improve the Retention of Biracial Students: A Case Study." *Journal of College Student Retention,* 2004, 5, 349–363.

Schmidt, P. "Federal Panel May Spur Changes in the Way Colleges Track Enrollment by Race." *Chronicle of Higher Education,* July 18, 1997, p. A27.

Skrentny, J. D. "Judges in U. of Michigan Case Skirted the Thorniest Issues." *Chronicle of Higher Education,* May 31, 2002, p. B20.

U.S. Department of Education. "Final Guidance on Maintaining, Collecting and Reporting Racial and Ethnic Data to the U.S. Department of Education." 2007. Retrieved Oct. 22, 2007, from http://edocket.access.gpo.gov/2007/pdf/E7-20613.pdf.

U.S. Office of Management and Budget. "Revisions to the Standards for the Classifica-
tion of Federal Data on Race and Ethnicity. 1997." Retrieved June 7, 2007, from
http://www.whitehouse.gov/omb/fedreg/ombdir15.html.
U.S. Office of Management and Budget. "Guidance on Aggregation and Allocation of
Data on Race for Use in Civil Rights Monitoring and Enforcement." 2000. Retrieved
Aug. 15, 2007, from http://www.whitehouse.gov/omb/bulletins/b00–02.html.
U.S. Office of Management and Budget. "Provisional Guidance on the Implementation
of the 1997 Standards for Federal Data on Race and Ethnicity." 2001. Retrieved Aug.
15, 2007, from http://www.whitehouse.gov/omb/inforeg/re_app-ctables.pdf.

ANGELA KELLOGG *works in the Student Academic Advising Center at the University of Wisconsin-Stevens Point. She has served as chair of the American College Personnel Association's Multiracial Network.*

AMANDA SUNITI NISKODÉ *is a doctoral candidate in the Higher Education and
Student Affairs Program at Indiana University (IU), Bloomington. She is a project associate at the National Survey of Student Engagement, IU Center for Postsecondary Research, and has served as chair of the American College Personnel
Association's Multiracial Network.*

NEW DIRECTIONS FOR STUDENT SERVICES • DOI: 10.1002/ss

INDEX

Act to Preserve Racial Integrity (1924) [Virginia], 7
Adelman, C., 9
Advisers: implications for students of bicultural, 79–80; multiracial student organizations and role of, 55. *See also* Faculty
Affirmative action, 98–100
African Americans: challenges faced by Black faculty, 76; "compulsory blackness" forced on, 84; "double consciousness" of, 74
American College Personnel Association: MultiRacial Network (MRN) of, 1, 43, 45, 56, 98; Standing Committee on Multicultural Affairs, 45
Appreciation level, 14, 18
Arnaz, D., 7
Association of Multi-Ethnic Americans, 59
Astin, A. W., 19
Atkinson, D., 13, 14, 15, 17
Attitudes: changing toward interracial couples, 8; of college students toward multiracial students, 44; improvement toward multiracial people in U.S., 44

Ball, L., 7
Bamaca, M. Y., 14, 20
Bannerji, H., 85, 90
Baysden, M., 33, 35
Bean, F. D., 23, 24
Bélanger, H., 88
Berry, H., 7
Berson, M. J., 7
Between: Living in the Hyphen (Nakagawa), 87
Bicultural faculty: biracial and bicultural experiences of, 74–76; Black, 76; faculty culture and, 76–78; impact on biracial and monoracial students by, 79–80; Native American, 80; racialization of, 78
"Bill of Rights for Multiracial Individuals" (Root), 68
Biracial college students: affirmative action and, 98–100; impact of bicultural faculty on, 79–80; new college diversity and, 8–9; post-affirmative action era and, 5–6; reorganizing insti-

tution assumptions about, 98; technology use by, 63–70; terminology/labels related to, 56; in the United States, 7–8. *See also* College students
Biracial identity: accessing personal biases about, 59; conflicts between advisor identity and student, 55–57; development, 14–16, 30–31, 44–45; study on self-labeling of, 23–31; understanding how others perceive, 59
Biracial identity development: challenges associated with, 30–31; impact of racism on, 15, 16; Internet facilitation of, 67; Poston's five level model on, 14–15; Root's model on resolutions of tensions of, 15–16; three types of, 44–45. *See also* Multiracial college students
Biracial identity study: background and implementation of, 23–24; implications of, 29–31; research methods used in, 23–26; results and findings of, 26–29
Biracial/bicultural commonalities, 74–76
Birnbaum, R., 76, 77, 78
Black Berry Sweet Juice: On Being Black and White in Canada (Hill), 86
Black faculty, 76
Blogging, 65–66
Bollinger, Grutter v., 98, 99, 100
Bonam, C., 14, 19, 20
"Border crossings," 30, 44, 45
Bracey, J. R., 14, 20
Broido, E. M., 9
Brown, U. M., 34, 36, 37, 38, 39
Brown University, 48–49, 50
Brunsma, D. L., 13, 14, 17, 19, 20
Buckner, J., 2, 43, 51
Bugeja, M., 69
Burleson, D. A., 67, 69
Bush, G. W., 6
Busher, H., 25

"Cablinasian" self-label, 28, 29, 56
CACI (Campus Awareness+Compliance Intitiative), 1, 56, 57, 58
Camper, C., 84
Campus: biracial and multiracial students' use of technology on, 66–68; racial politics of, 58, 67; technology trends on, 63–66. *See also* Institutions